ROUTLEDGE LIBRARY EDITIONS:
FINANCIAL MARKETS

Volume 13

ISSUES IN INTERNATIONAL CAPITAL MOBILITY

ISSUES IN INTERNATIONAL CAPITAL MOBILITY

HELEN A. POPPER

LONDON AND NEW YORK

First published in 1997 by Garland Publishing, Inc.

This edition first published in 2018
by Routledge
2 Park Square, Milton Park, Abingdon, Oxon OX14 4RN

and by Routledge
711 Third Avenue, New York, NY 10017

Routledge is an imprint of the Taylor & Francis Group, an informa business

British Library Cataloguing in Publication Data
A catalogue record for this book is available from the British Library

ISBN: 978-1-138-56537-1 (Set)
ISBN: 978-0-203-70248-2 (Set) (ebk)
ISBN: 978-1-138-56673-6 (Volume 13) (hbk)
ISBN: 978-1-138-56681-1 (Volume 13) (pbk)
ISBN: 978-1-315-12387-5 (Volume 13) (ebk)

Publisher's Note
The publisher has gone to great lengths to ensure the quality of this reprint but points out that some imperfections in the original copies may be apparent.

ISSUES IN INTERNATIONAL CAPITAL MOBILITY

HELEN A. POPPER

GARLAND PUBLISHING, INC.
NEW YORK & LONDON / 1997

Much of Chapter 2 is reprinted from the *Journal of International Money and Finance* (12:4, © 1993) with the kind permission of Elsevier Science, Ltd. Much of Chapter 3 is reprinted from the *Open Economics Review* (Vol. 6, © 1995) with the kind permission of Kluwer Academic Publishers.

Library of Congress Cataloging-in-Publication Data

Popper, Helen Ann.
Issues in international capital mobility / Helen A. Popper.
p. cm. — (Financial sector of the American economy)
Includes bibliographical references and index.
ISBN 0-8153-2817-6 (alk. paper)
1. Capital movements. 2. Capital market. I. Title.
II. Series.
HG3891.P66 1997
332'.042—dc21

97-495

Printed on acid-free, 250-year-life paper
Manufactured in the United States of America

For Mom.

Contents

Tables ix
Preface xi
Acknowledgments xv

I. Gauging International Capital Mobility 3

II. Long-Term Covered Interest Parity Evidence from Currency Swaps 15

III. Term Premia Comovement in German, Japanese, and U.S. Domestic Markets 37

Term Premia Appendix 57

IV. Formulating Non-Linear Moment Conditions for Generalized Method of Moments Estimators 67

References 83

Index 89

Tables

Table 1	Euromarket Long-Term Swap-Covered Interest Parity Deviations	22
Table 2	Onshore Markets' Long-Term Swap-Covered Interest Parity Deviations	24
Table 3	Onshore Markets' Short-Term Swap-Covered Interest Parity Deviations	25
Table 4	Probability Values	34
Table 5	Variance Ratio	35
Table 6	Unrestricted Term Premia Estimates	44
Table 7	Term Premia Comovement	45
Table 8	Hypothesis Tests	47
Table 9	Constant Risk Premium	48
Table 10	Multiplicative Hypothesis Formulation	59
Table 11	Proportionate Hypothesis Formulation	60
Table 12	Monte Carlo Simulations	62
Table 13	Generalized Method of Moments Estimates	63
Table 14	GMM Estimates	75

Preface

The answers to many questions in international finance and economics depend on the degree of openness of international capital markets. Unfortunately, the openness of capital markets is not easy to gauge. Openness varies from country to country, and it varies across time. Moreover, there are many competing methods for gauging the degree of international capital mobility, and the conclusions drawn from these competing methods often conflict. The result is that informed statements about the degree of international capital mobility typically are circumspect.

The most concrete statements usually are made about short-term assets that are traded in the Euromarket. In that market, financial capital flows essentially are unrestricted. Moving away from the Euromarket, into the domestic market of industrialized and developing countries, assets become more heterogeneous, and assessments of market integration become increasingly complicated. Empirical investigations encompassing broader ranges of assets or of markets have been correspondingly more involved, and their conclusions have been less definitive.

In three related studies, this book addresses a few of the ambiguities arising in empirical investigations of capital market openness. It does this by taking existing empirical approaches and adapting them to new markets and to new assets. It also examines the properties of one statistical method used to assess the extent of international capital mobility. While each study can be read on its own, collectively they reinforce the notion that the financial markets of industrialized countries are very well integrated--notwithstanding the sometimes substantial differences in returns to risky assets. The three studies stem from my Ph.D. dissertation, written at the University of California at Berkeley. The additional results, not included in the dissertation itself, primarily reflect responses to the anonymous referees who generously provided extensive comments.

In its first chapter, the book briefly discusses some recent financial market liberalizations that have affected the extent of international capital mobility. The chapter begins with a broad overview of the approaches used to assess the extent of international capital mobility. Among the most important approaches have been examinations of the cost of capital across countries. Interest rate parity conditions embody the notion that the cost of capital should be closely linked when markets are open, and the parity conditions are described at some length. The results of various parity studies are also described. Another important approach to gauging the extent of international capital mobility stems from an examination of the links between various non-financial economic variables, most importantly, saving and investment. Studies of saving and investment behavior and their implications for openness also are described.

In Chapter 2, one of the interest rate parity conditions is extended from the realm of short-term assets to that of long-term assets. Currency swaps are used to construct long-term international transactions that cover for exchange rate risk. The "swap-covered" interest parity conditions are used to show that short-term and long-term assets are equally mobile across many markets. The swap-covered returns are compared both in the Euromarket and across the domestic markets of the United States and five other industrialized countries, Canada, Germany, Japan, Switzerland, and the United Kingdom. The evidence shows that, among these countries, the barriers to the mobility of financial capital, even at the long end of the maturity spectrum, are minor.

In Chapter 3, a more general model, the latent variable model, is used to assess the extent of the co-movement of the term premia across the domestic markets of the United States, Germany and Japan. Like the assets examined in Chapter 2, the term premia examined here differ with regard to their original currency of denomination and political jurisdiction. However, unlike the covered assets of Chapter 2, the assets examined here are risky, and they differ in their riskiness. Ex post term premia depend on fluctuations in both interest rates and exchange rates. The latent variable model is used as a framework for examining whether or not these risky returns are priced similarly across markets. The evidence presented in Chapter 3 supports the hypothesis that the term premia behave as if they exist in a single market.

The last chapter investigates an econometric issue associated with the empirical evaluation of many asset pricing models commonly used to address the issue of capital market integration, as well as in a variety of other types of empirical studies. Chapter 4 shows that estimates arising from the technique of generalized method of moments are sensitive to the specific formulation chosen to represent a given hypothesis. That is, the parameter estimates arising from the use of generalized method of moment estimators are not unique when non-linear transformation of the orthogonal conditions are allowed. This sensitivity of the parameter estimates is demonstrated empirically using the latent variable model and data of Chapter 3.

Acknowledgments

I am grateful for the guidance provided by my thesis advisors, Roger Craine, Jeffrey Frankel, and Greg Connor. I also would like to thank Charles Pigott, Bruce Kasman, and Ken Weiller for encouraging the development of the currency swap study, initiated while I was visiting the International Research Department of the Federal Reserve Bank of New York. Discussions with my fellow graduate students from Berkeley were also very helpful. In particular, I would like to thank Alan MacArthur for early discussions of interest parity conditions and Joe Mattey for programing suggestions for use in Monte Carlo work. The latter chapters were written while I was at the Federal Reserve Board, and many of my colleagues there, among them, Hali Edison and Neil Ericsson, also provided helpful discussions and comments. Salomon Brothers Inc. generously supplied the currency swap data. My most important thanks go to my husband, Douglas Gottschlich, for his continual encouragement. The views expressed here are my own and do not necessarily reflect those of the Federal Reserve Bank of New York or of the Federal Reserve System.

Issues in International Capital Mobility

Chapter 1

Gauging International Capital Mobility

How open are international capital markets? The answer to this question depends on the applicable benchmark of "openness." One benchmark may be the extent of mobility within the confines of a single country. We can ask, for example: does capital move as freely within Europe as it does within the U.S.A.? Another benchmark is the degree of openness at a particular point in history. It is often argued that capital markets were open in the late nineteenth century. Are they as open today? Answering these questions in turn requires an empirical measure of openness that can be applied across countries and across time.

Economists have used two approaches to measure the openness of international capital markets, and each approach has its own limitations. The first approach relies on an examination of the quantity of capital flowing from one country to another. Capital flows suggests capital mobility. Similarly, some argue, a lack of flows may indicate a barrier to mobility. Of course, a lack of flows, by itself, does not provide conclusive evidence of a barrier. Just as a lamb may stay in its own green pasture with or without a fence, a country's capital may remain within its borders if no return differential induces capital's movement across borders. Despite this limitation, the technique of assessing capital mobility by examining the capital flows themselves has remained prominent for almost twenty years.

The second approach to measuring the openness of international capital markets examines international rates of return to capital. Large differences in the returns to comparable assets cannot exist if capital can move freely across markets. Countries with high returns will attract capital from those with low returns until the return difference diminishes. Thus, return differences on comparable assets provide evidence of barriers to capital mobility. Of course, critical to this approach is the ability to find assets that can be compared internationally. Assets differ in terms of the currencies in which they are denominated, in terms of their maturities and other aspects of their payment structures, and in terms of the prospects of their issuers. Anything that causes two assets to differ in terms of their relevant risk characteristics should correspondingly cause their returns to differ, even within a single market. Thus, the rate of return approach must adequately account for the potential differences in the underlying assets. Otherwise, even perfectly integrated markets might appear as if they were segmented.

As capital markets have become increasingly well integrated since the 1980s, both the quantity-based and the rate-of-return based approaches have evolved. This chapter first briefly reviews some of the recent financial market changes that are suggestive of increasing international integration. Then it surveys the advances in the use of the quantity based and rate of return based approaches to assessing the extent of that integration.

RECENT FINANCIAL DEREGULATION

The last several decades have brought sweeping reforms of the capital markets around the world. Integration of the financial markets of many industrialized countries accelerated in the mid-eighties. Withholding taxes on interest payments to nonresidents were abolished in the United States, making foreign holdings of U.S. bonds suddenly more attractive. Soon after, France, Germany, and the United Kingdom also abolished withholding taxes and otherwise liberalized their markets.[1] In 1992, Europeans removed most of the remaining official impediments to the free movement of capital within Europe. In Japan, an important financial liberalization package, introduced in the mid-eighties, brought about the development of new domestic and offshore money markets in subsequent years.[2] More recently, Japanese officials have announced their intention to dismantle many of the remaining domestic financial regulations that have been seen as an effective barrier to market integration.

Financial liberalization has been less synchronized and often less sweeping outside of the most-industrialized countries. Nevertheless, many barries to capital mobility have been lifted in Asia, in Latin America, and, of course, in Eastern Europe. For example, Indonesia substantially liberalized its treatment of both domestic and foreign capital in the early eighties.[3] Korea introduced some liberalization measures and accelarated interest rate decontrol in the late eighties.[4] India removed many of its stringent barriers to capital inflows in the early nineties. In Latin America, many financial markets were opened up to foreigners in the late eighties and early nineties as many Latin American countries liberalized their markets as part of broader stabilization packages.[5]

These wide-spread and far-reaching liberalizations certainly enhance capital market integration. Yet, we do not know by how much. The changed regulations alone do not tell us if markets are now well enough integrated so that assets can be viewed as trading within a single international market (or even within a single European market). Remaining official barriers, unofficial, *de facto*, barriers, and the latent threat of new--or renewed--capital constraints all still may limit the movement of capital in important ways. Both the quantity-based approaches and the rate-of-return based approaches provide a means to discerning whether effective barriers, official or not, remain in place.

SAVING AND INVESTMENT CORRELATIONS

One of the most important of the quantity-based approaches owes its prominence to the work of Feldstein and Horioka (1980), who investigated the links between domestic saving and investment. Feldstein and Horioka emphasized that barriers to international capital mobility imply that domestic investment must be financed with domestic saving. In a country with a completely closed capital market, domestic saving must equal domestic investment. In contrast, if capital markets are open, domestic investment opportunities will draw in capital from abroad; and domestic saving can finance investment abroad. Feldstein and Horioka examined the empirical link between saving and investment in OECD countries. They estimated an equation describing investment as a function of saving. Surprising many economists at the time, they found saving and investment to be highly correlated. Feldstein and Horioka estimate the following equation:

$$i_j = \beta s_j + u_j,$$

where i_j and s_j represent a country's (country j) saving and investment a fraction of GNP over five years. They found estimates of β to be close to one. They then interpreted their finding as evidence of substantial barriers to capital mobility.

Their work received a barrage of econometric criticisms. Most important among the criticisms has been the argument that the high correlation reflected omitted variables that simultaneously determined both investment and saving. Demographic and political factors can cause increases or decreases in both the domestic saving and the domestic investment of a country. As a consequence, the two series would move together even in the absence of any impediments to capital mobility.[6] Simultaneity remains a problem even when Feldstein and Horioka's approach is modified to examine a single country over time. When such a time series is used instead of a cross section of countries, the problem of simultaneity can be introduced through the business cycle. Whether through interest rates or through some other mechanism, the business cycle arguably can affect saving and investment together, with or without barriers to capital mobility.

Additional studies by many scholars have failed to resolve the simultaneity problem, but neither have they seriously shaken the finding of saving and investment's high correlation across countries. The finding is a robust one.[7] As Taylor (1995) points out, the correlation does vary through time and from one country to another. Nevertheless, cross sectional estimates of β have been closer to one than to zero throughout most of this century.[8]

While the empirical link between saving and investment is now evident, the interpretation is not correspondingly clear. We know, for example, that there have been gross flows of capital across borders at the same time. Moreover, for many countries, capital flows have taken every possible form. The link between saving and investment corresponds most closely with the behavior of net flows, not gross flows. Yet, large gross flows can be indicative of open markets, regardless of the small size of net flows.[9] Also seeming to contradict Feldstein and Horioka's interpretation is the considerable evidence that returns are linked internationally. Regarding this, Feldstein and Horioka wrote:

> It is clear from the yields on short-term securities in the Eurocurrency market and the forward prices of those currencies that liquid financial capital moves very rapidly to arbitrage such short-term international yield differentials. Unfortunately, similar measures of

> expected real net-of-tax yields on long-term portfolio capital or direct investments cannot be observed.

They conclude that "most capital is apparently not available for such arbitrage-type activity among long-term investments." One of the things that made Feldstein and Horioka's work as important as it was in 1980 was that it was difficult at that time to test whether or not they were right about long-term arbitrage. Now, however, we can examine more carefully both the short-term and the long term links between the returns of different countries.

INTEREST RATE PARITY

The degree of capital market integration should be reflected by the extent to which yields on similar assets are in some sense equivalent across markets. That interest rates may be equivalent in a number of senses is indicated by the various definitions of interest rate parity: nominal interest parity, real interest parity, uncovered interest parity, and covered interest parity.

The concept of nominal interest parity simply equates the domestic nominal interest rate, r_t, with the foreign nominal interest rate, $r^*_{t,\ t+s}$, over any given time interval, t to t+s. Of course, when inflation in the two countries differs and exchange rates are expected to change, there is no reason for nominal parity to hold. Inflation differences are captured by the notion of real interest parity:

Real Interest Parity:
$$\frac{1 + r_{t,\ t+s}}{1 + \pi_{t,\ t+s}} = \frac{1 + r^*_{t,\ t+s}}{1 + \pi^*_{t,\ t+s}}$$

where, $\pi_{t,\ t+s}$ and $\pi^*_{t,\ t+s}$ are the domestic and foreign inflation rates. The real interest rate parity condition has been rejected in even the most open of markets. Frankel (1991) emphasizes that the rejection should not be sunrising: Purchasing power parity typically does not hold; and, without purchasing power parity, real interest parity should not hold. Moreover, real interest parity is not an arbitrage condition, so deviations from real interest parity do not necessarily induce capital to flow immediately. As a consequence, real interest parity does not provide a clear gauge of capital market integration.

As an alternative to adjusting returns for inflation, they can be adjusted for expected exchange rate changes. Expected appreciation or depreciation can be incorporated using the uncovered interest parity condition:

$$\textit{Uncovered Interest Parity:}\quad 1 + r_{t,\,t+s} = \frac{S_t(1 + r^*_{t,\,t+s})}{E_t(S_{t+s})}$$

where S_t is the spot exchange rate in period t, and is given in units of foreign currency per domestic currency; and $E_t(s_{t+s})$ is the expected spot exchange rate in period $t+s$. Using realized depreciation in lieu of expected depreciation, empirical tests have overwhelmingly rejected the joint hypothesis of uncovered interest parity and rational expectations. While uncovered interest parity incorporates expected changes in exchange rates, holding a foreign asset nevertheless leaves an investor open to exchange rate risk. Thus, uncovered interest parity requires at least either completely diversifiable risk, or risk neutral investors.

Persistent differences between interest rates, after adjusting for expected depreciation, have been attributed to exchange rate risk, to transaction costs, and to political risk, where political risk encompasses both existing capital controls and expected capital controls. To distinguish among some of these components, tests of covered interest parity have been used. Covered interest parity uses a forward exchange contract to remove exchange rate risk.

The covered interest parity condition can be written as:

$$\textit{Covered Interest Parity:} \quad 1 + r_{t,\,t+s} = \frac{S_t(1 + r^*_{t,\,t+s})}{F_{t,\,t+s}}$$

where $F_{t,\,t+s}$ is the forward rate contracted at period t for currency exchange at period t + s, and it is expressed here in units of foreign currency per unit of domestic currency. By abstracting from exchange rate risk, tests for deviations from covered interest parity measure whether political risk and transaction costs are large enough to act as barriers to international capital mobility.

The covered interest parity condition has been examined extensively using short-term instruments. For many markets, covered interest parity holds quite closely. This indicates that those capital markets are now well integrated. In other markets, and at other times, deviations from covered interest parity can be quite large. Frankel and McArthur (1988) document both situations. They find only small deviations from covered interest parity in some markets, and deviations of as much as several hundred basis points in other markets. The smallest deviations are found within the Euromarket, where individual countries are largely unable to impose capital controls effectively.

Because of the relatively early development of the short-term forward contracts, the covered interest parity condition has been applied predominantly to the short-term market. Until the evolution of similar financial instruments for hedging the foreign exchange exposure of long-term assets, the condition could not be applied to examine the equivalence of long-term returns. In the absence of such instruments, one could gauge capital mobility by comparing the returns of assets denominated in the same currency but issued in different markets. For example, to gauge the openness of the German bond market, one could compare the return on a long-term, mark-denominated bond issued in Germany with the return to a mark-denominated bond issued in the Euromarket. A finding of pervasive differences in the returns would suggest that there were barriers between the German market and the Euromarket. Such differences have indeed been found, not only between the German market and the Euromarket, but between other markets as well. Unfortunately, the differences could not be interpreted unambiguously as indicators of barriers to capital mobility. The ambiguity reflects the difficulty of ruling out the possibility that the differences corresponded to differences in the attributes of the bonds issued in the various markets.

Only recently has the covered interest parity condition been extended to examine long-term returns. Chapter 2, which was originally published in the *Journal of International Finance*, presents the first such application. It shows how a cross-currency interest rate swap can be used to construct a comparable long-term covered interest parity condition. The condition is examined for a set of industrialized countries for which short-term deviations have been found to be quite small. As described in Chapter 2, the long-term deviations from covered interest parity also are found to be small--roughly the size of their short-term counterparts. Subsequent work by Takezawa (1995) applies the same approach using daily data, and Takezawa also finds that recent deviations have been small.

These interest parity approaches, whether they examine short-term assets or long-term assets, share one drawback. Each interest parity condition embodies a narrow treatment of risk. Covered interest parity, for example, says nothing about the behavior of risky returns. So, it provides only a minimum requirement for a finding of market integration. Meanwhile, uncovered interest parity treats returns as though risk were irrelevant, so it is too strong a condition for evaluating market integration. Determining whether risky assets that are issued in potentially distinct markets are priced as though they are traded in a single market calls for an asset pricing model that embraces risk. While the interest parity conditions described here have provided a mainstay for studying barriers to capital mobility, more general models, such as the one used in Chapter 3, can more fully embrace risk. Thus, they potentially can provide a richer understanding of international capital market integration.

NOTES

1. In 1985 and 1986, Germany removed restrictions on the form of foreign borrowing in German markets; France lifted its restriction that French residents only purchase foreign assets from other French residents; and the United Kingdom liberalized its security markets with it's "Big Bang."

2. New short-term markets included the uncollateralized call money market in 1985, the treasury bill market in 1986, and the commercial paper market and the Tokyo offshore money market in 1987. Over the same period, foreign companies were allowed to begin Japanese banking and securities operations. Shigehara (1990) provides a succinct summary of these and other Japanese financial market liberalizations occurring in the eighties.

3. While financial markets were liberalized early in Indonesia, trade restrictions were not eased until later in the decade. See Thorbecke (1992) for more details.

4. Several major commercial banks were privatized in Korea in 1982, and in 1984 some restrictions on interest rates were removed. For more a more detailed discussion of the Korean liberalization, see Frankel (1992).

5. Paredes (1991) summarizes the dramitic changes of the Fujimori government in 1990.

6. Arguing that the correlation may be an artifact of factors simultaneously affecting saving and investment, Summers (1988) points to population growth as an example. He also provides the "maintained external balance hypothesis:" Saving and investment may move together as a result of economic policy reactions taken by sovereign states in response to unbalanced current accounts."

7. See, for example, Obstfeld (1986,1994), Frankel (1991), Tesar (1991), and Taylor (1995).

8. While Taylor reports a wide range of time-series results outside of the United States, he reports U.S. estimates close to one for most of this century.

9. Of course, even if we observe some gross flows, there nevertheless may be some market impediments that cause capital

to move less that it otherwise would. That is, what we may be seeing is the combination of some capital constraints and capital flows that, whatever their magnitude, are less than they would be were the constraints removed. To determine whether this is the case, we need some benchmark for how much the flows would be in perfectly integrated world markets. Lewis (1994) discusses two approaches that provide some insight into what would be a suitable benchmark. In describing the "home bias" puzzle, she observes that individuals hold insufficient foreign assets relative to what is predicted by the capital asset pricing model and by an explicit model of international consumption risk sharing.

Chapter 2

Long-Term Covered Interest Parity Evidence from Currency Swaps

While most economists would agree that international financial markets have become increasingly integrated over the past decade, consensus regarding the extent of integration has been limited to the realm of short-term asset markets, and sometimes only to the Euromarket. For many economic questions, the behavior of long-term financial capital is more relevant, and the integration of financial markets across different political jurisdictions is often critical.[1] This chapter provides explicit measures of the international mobility of long-term financial capital across bond markets that are potentially distinct. Interest arbitrage conditions previously applied only to short-term assets are used to compare long-term bond yields both within the Euromarket and across the onshore markets of Canada, Japan, Germany, Switzerland, the United Kingdom, and the United States. The evidence provide here indicates that long-term financial capital is as mobile in these markets as is short-term capital. This appears to be the case both within the Euromarket and across political jurisdictions.

The long-term arbitrage conditions are constructed using a now well-developed mechanism for hedging long-term currency positions, the cross-currency interest rate swap, usually called a *currency swap.* (The currency swap is distinct from the *foreign exchange swap,* which has been traded in the interbank market for many years and underlies short-term forward foreign exchange trading.) The longer-term currency swap consists of an exchange of a stream of interest payments in one currency for a stream of payments in another currency. In many ways, it is equivalent to a series of forward contracts. It is used here to abstract from currency risk to compare long-term bond yields.

The next section of this chapter briefly reviews the results of some of the major studies of interest arbitrage among short-term assets. Analogous arbitrage measures for long-term yields using currency swaps are presented in the subseqent section. Next, the data used to derive these measures are described. The long-term measures are then applied to examine the Euromarket, and the markets of Canada, Germany, Japan, Switzerland, and the United Kingdom. Measures of the extent of deviations from parity are presented and compared with short-term deviations from parity. Finally, the chapter concludes with a brief interpretation of the findings.

SHORT-TERM COVERED INTEREST PARITY

Persistent differences across international boundaries between realized returns on comparable assets have been attributed most importantly to exchange rate risk and political risk, where political risk encompasses both existing and expected capital controls related to the political jurisdiction of issue.[2] Forward foreign exchange contracts remove exchange rate risk and allow returns to be compared in an arbitrage condition. The arbitrage condition, covered interest parity, equates the domestic-currency return with a fully hedged foreign-currency return:

$$(1) \qquad (1 + r_{t,t+s}) = (1 + r^*_{t,t+s}) \cdot \frac{S_t}{F_{t,t+s}}$$

In Equation 1, $r_{t,\,t+s}$ is the domestic currency rate of return from period t to period t + s, $r^*_{t,\,t+s}$ is the foreign currency rate of return over the same period, S_t is the foreign currency price of a domestic currency unit at period t, and $F_{t,\,t+s}$ is the forward exchange rate contracted at period t for exchange at period t + s.[3]

Measures of covered interest parity until now have involved only short-term assets. The smallest deviations from short-term covered interest parity have been found in the Euromarket, where political risk is the same regardless of currency. Carefully synchronizing daily Euromarket observations for six months, Clinton (1988) found that 95 percent of the deviations were less than about 20 basis points in absolute value, and most of the deviations averaged only a few basis points.[4] Taylor (1987) sampled Euromarket rates at 10 minute intervals and also found deviations from parity to be very small.[5]

Measured interest disparities are often larger across onshore markets (and between onshore and offshore markets). This primarily reflects the political risk that can exist in onshore markets, although one also expects greater measurement error across onshore markets. As political risk varies across countries and time periods, observed onshore interest disparities can vary considerably. For example, among the countries they termed "Open Developed Countries," Frankel and MacArthur (1988) found disparities with sample standard deviations and root mean square errors ranging from about 20 basis points to about 50 basis points.[6] Giavazzi and Pagano (1985) found similar disparities in Dutch and German markets.[7] In contrast, the same studies showed disparities with sample standard deviations and root mean square errors of several hundred basis points among the "Other European Developed Countries" and "Closed Less Developed

Countries" of Frankel and MacArthur and in the French and Italian markets examined by Giavazzi and Pagano.[8] Mean disparity measures show a similar pattern.[9]

CURRENCY SWAP-COVERED INTEREST PARITY

The exclusive attention given to short-term asset returns reflects the relative development of short-term and long-term international financial markets. Most importantly for the use of covered interest parity, explicit forward exchange contracts and the foreign exchange swaps are well-traded only at short maturities, making direct covered interest parity measures inapplicable to long-term assets.[10] Both forward contracts and foreign exchange swap contracts are most developed at the three-month maturity and are extremely costly at maturities greater than two years, even among the most commonly traded currencies. Because the linkages between short-term and long-term returns in the same currency are not well established, and because capital controls are sometimes not applied uniformly across maturities, short-term covered interest parity is not sufficient to guarantee interest parity among long-term assets.

Only recently has the currency swap market become sufficiently developed to provide the necessary long-term counterpart to the covered interest parity condition. Currency swaps are now well traded instruments with outstandings exceeding $300 billion by the end of 1988.[11] Like a forward contract, a currency swap allows a domestic investor to hold a foreign-currency denominated asset without currency risk on the invested principal. The mechanics of a currency swap differ from that of a forward contract or a foreign exchange swap in that a currency swap contract is an agreement to exchange over time a *stream* of payments in one currency for a *stream* of payments in another, while forward contracts and foreign exchange swaps are agreements to exchange fixed amounts of two currencies at a single future date.[12] Typically, a currency swap payment stream mimics that of a bond. Currency swaps enable borrowers to arbitrage the long-term returns of assets denominated in different currencies.

At standard maturities, the price of a currency swap is conventionally quoted as a stream of fixed non-dollar payments against a stream of floating dollar payments. To compare *fixed* interest rates in a way analogous to covered interest parity, the currency swap must be combined with an interest rate swap, which converts the floating dollar rate into a fixed rate.[13]

Once the dollar portion of the currency swap is converted into a fixed interest rate, it and the non-dollar currency swap return can be used to construct the swap-covered interest parity condition. As with short-term covered interest parity, the swap-parity condition comes from equating a domestic currency return with a comparable covered foreign-currency return. An investor may either invest in a domestic currency asset and earn the per-period return, $r_{t,\,t+s}$, or invest abroad and cover for exchange rate risk with a currency swap.

The swap-covered foreign return is the sum of the uncovered foreign-currency return and the net currency swap payments.[14] Denote the fixed dollar rate exchanged in the currency swap as $r_{t,\,t+s}^{sw}$, and denote the fixed non-dollar rate exchanged in the currency swap as $r_{t,\,t+s}^{sw*}$. In the completed foreign transaction, the investor earns the per-period uncovered foreign-currency return, $r_{t,\,t+s}^{*}$, while paying the foreign-currency swap rate, $r_{t,\,t+s}^{sw*}$ and receiving the domestic-currency swap rate, $r_{t,\,t+s}^{sw}$. Thus, the net foreign covered return is:

$$r_{t,\,t+s}^{*} + r_{t,\,t+s}^{sw} - r_{t,\,t+s}^{sw*}.$$

Arbitrage equates the two returns and gives a swap-covered interest parity condition:[15]

$$(2) \qquad r_{t,\,t+s} - (r^{*}_{t,\,t+s} + r^{sw}_{t,\,t+s} - r^{sw*}_{t,\,t+s}) = 0$$

The swap-covered parity condition is evaluated in this chapter first among assets denominated in different currencies but issued in the Euromarket, where political risk should be unimportant. It is evaluated next among onshore markets, where political risk may play a role. Deviations from long-term swap-covered parity, Equation 2, are measured, and they are also compared with deviations from the short-term covered interest parity counterpart, Equation 1.

As discussed in the short-term context, covered interest rate disparities in principle are attributed to the existence of either political risk or transaction costs. In practice, observed deviations from parity may also be due both to non-comparability of assets and to measurement error. In this chapter, while assets as homogeneous as possible are chosen, they are not identical and may suffer from differential default risk, particularly in the Euromarket.[16] Neither are all prices sampled at precisely the same instant. Bond and swap yields are measured at the close of each market.[17] Finally, measurement error also arises from the use of estimated bond yields and other yield approximations.[18] Because of these errors, some deviations from parity may be observed even when capital is perfectly mobile. In this chapter, the importance of the observed deviations is evaluated by considering them in the context of their short-term counterparts that have been studied in a variety of markets. First, the data are described.

Data

The long-term swap-covered interest parity condition, Equation 2, is evaluated using assets with maturities of five years and seven years. The U.S. dollar serves as the domestic currency. The foreign currencies used are those of Canada, Germany, Japan, Switzerland, and the United Kingdom. Cross-currency interest rate swap quotes and bond yields were provided by Salomon Brothers and are published in their *International Bond Market Roundup.* Interest rate swap prices were provided by Fulton Prebon Inc.

Short-term covered interest parity, Equation 1, is examined across onshore markets using three-month assets. The short-term onshore rates are: the interbank rates in Germany, Switzerland, and the United Kingdom; the finance paper rate in Canada; the Gensaki rate in Japan; and the ninety-day Federal Funds rate in the United States.

The sample period extends from October 3, 1985 to February 18, 1988 for the long-term onshore bond yields and for all the short-term measures.[19] The starting point varies slightly among Eurobonds: for mark-denominated Eurobonds, the sample begins October 3, 1985; for Eurobonds denominated in Canadian dollars, sterling, and Swiss francs, it begins November 28, 1985; and, for yen-denominated Eurobonds, it begins November 13, 1986. Observations are taken on the Thursday of each week.

Empirical Results

The interesting empirical question is whether the observed deviations from swap-covered parity are large in the sense of being indicative either of market inefficiency or of barriers to capital mobility among long-term assets. One way to help judge the importance of the long-term deviations that are observed here

Table 1
Euromarket

Long-Term Swap-Covered Interest Parity Deviations
(in basis points, annual returns)

	Mean absolute deviation (a)	Sample s.d. (b)	Root mean square error (c)	95 percent band (d)	Mean (e)
Canadian Dollar					
5 year	29.77	38.41	38.45	-69.50, 65.00	-2.41
7 year	31.13	39.80	40.19	-39.00, 67.00	4.70
Mark					
5 year	18.80	25.43	25.63	-45.10, 57.50	3.15
7 year	22.60	26.77	27.88	-52.87, 39.50	-7.54
Yen					
5 year	21.95	26.26	29.65	-32.00, 71.50	13.97
7 year	27.78	27.92	33.34	-41.50, 67.00	18.53
Sterling					
5 year	28.89	35.32	37.03	-64.00, 74.67	13.22
7 year	n.a.	n.a.	n.a.	n.a.	n.a.
Swiss Franc					
5 year	14.90	22.05	22.26	-44.50, 43.50	-3.06
7 year	13.60	21.94	21.98	-43.00, 47.00	-1.78
Average	22.33	28.55	29.69		2.84

1. Sample Periods: Mark-denominated Eurobonds: 123 observations, October 3, 1985 to February 18, 1988.
   Sterling, Swiss, and 5-year Canadian Eurobonds: 115 observations, November 28, 1985 to February 18, 1988.
   Yen-denominated Eurobonds: 67 observations, November 13, 1986 to February 18, 1988.
   Canadian Dollar 7-year Eurobonds: 35 observations, May 28, 1987 to February 18, 1988.
2. Averages are weighted by the sample size.

is to compare them with corresponding short-term measures. To the extent that the markets examined here are characterized by mobility among short-term assets, yet disparities of some size are nevertheless observed, these observed short-term disparities implicitly define a range of deviations from parity that may be viewed as being consistent with capital mobility. Thus, the long-term and short-term disparities are evaluated together. In judging the importance of the measured disparities, is also useful to consider their size in relation to the size of disparities found in earlier (short-term) studies of markets where political risk did appear to be a concern. So, the results of these earlier studies are noted as well.

The disparity measures are summarized in Tables 1 through 3. Several measures are provided, including mean absolute deviations and some variability measures: the sample standard deviation, the root mean square error, and the size of the band needed to encompass 95 percent of the deviations from parity. Mean disparities are also given in the tables, but the mean is not emphasized in the discussion since, by itself, it may be a misleading statistic. Most importantly, the mean may be deceptively close to zero if large individual deviations of opposite sign partially offset one another in the sample period. Moreover,high estimates of the variance, while indicative of economically important deviations in individual periods, lead to findings of statistical insignificance of the means. Because of this problem, the assessment of the long-term interest disparities emphasizes the mean *absolute* deviations and measures of variability.[20]

The mean absolute deviations among the long-term assets in the Euromarket are given in the first column of Table 1; and the mean absolute deviations in the onshore markets are given in the first column of Table 2. Those of the short-term assets are given in Column (a) of Table 3.[21] In the short-term markets, in the long-term Euromarkets, and in the long-term Canadian, Japanese, and Swiss onshore markets, the mean absolute deviations range

Table 2
Onshore Markets

Long-Term Swap-Covered Interest Parity Deviations
(in basis points, annual returns)

	Mean absolute deviation (a)	Sample s.d. (b)	Root mean square error (c)	95 percent band (d)	Mean (e)
Canadian Dollar					
5 year	15.12	24.10	25.95	-40.90, 48.70	5.13
7 year	15.73	24.93	25.59	-31.00, 31.08	5.68
Mark					
5 year	48.30	33.78	55.04	-64.10, 95.00	44.97
7 year	42.19	32.19	46.35	67.50, 72.00	35.57
Yen					
5 year	26.15	32.09	33.38	-65.00, 58.50	9.75
7 year	27.15	30.99	33.39	-55.50, 60.50	13.61
Sterling					
5 year	49.75	41.15	63.70	-40.00, 82.00	48.46
7 year	46.58	31.67	55.74	-27.30, 80.00	46.21
Swiss Franc					
5 year	22.04	29.64	29.65	-55.50, 53.66	10.97
7 year	27.41	32.11	34.42	-60.00, 38.50	-11.41
					20.89
Average	32.04	31.27	40.32		

Note: The sample periods extends from October 3, 1985 to February 18, 1988.

Table 3

Onshore Markets

Short-Term Covered Interest Parity Deviations

(in basis points, annual returns)

	Mean absolute deviation (a)	Sample s.d. (b)	Root mean square error (c)	95 percent band (d)	Mean (e)
Canadian Dollar	13.89	15.67	60.51	-34.86, 40.75	1.57
Mark	29.20	16.65	33.13	-58.69, 10.78	-28.64
Yen	28.63	36.50	37.24	-64.29, 74.65	-7.38
Sterling	14.84	21.32	22.27	-33.16, 39.49	6.44
Swiss Franc	26.34	33.89	38.05	-64.41, 59.61	-17.31
Average	22.58	24.81	38.24		-9.06

Note: The sample periods extends from October 3, 1985 to February 18, 1988.

from about 15 basis points to about 30 basis points. They are only slightly higher in the long-term German and U.K. markets,where they reach about 50 basis points. Overall, the mean absolute deviations average about 10 basis points higher among the long-term assets than among the short-term assets. None of the mean absolute deviations are statistically different from zero.[22]

It is difficult to directly compare these measures (either short-term or long-term) with many earlier covered interest parity studies since mean absolute deviations aren't reported in many of them. However, the measures given here are comparable to those of Giavazzi and Pagano (1985) who report the means of disparities of the *same sign* for short-term deviations from parity. In the countries and periods most free of capital controls, their measures of disparity fall in the same range as that of both the short-term and long-term markets examined here, about 15 basis points to about 50 basis points.[23] However, they find that the evidence form countries and periods where capital controls are a concern provides a stark contrast. For those countries, Giavazzi and Pagano report (same sign) mean deviations of several hundred basis points. In the context of such large interest disparities, the long-term mean absolute disparities found here appear to be relatively small and not very different from their short-term counterparts.

The next three columns of Tables 1 through 3 present the interest disparities in terms of their variability: their sample standard deviations, root mean square errors, and the size of the bands necessary to encompass 95 percent of the deviations from parity. By these measures, the long-term disparities again are not considerably larger than the short-term disparities. Sample standard deviations from interest parity are given in the second column (Column b) of each table. Overall, the average sample standard deviations differ by less than 10 basis points between the long-term and short-term maturities. The sample standard deviations among the long-term assets average close to 30 basis points, and the sample standard deviations of the short-term differentials average about 25 basis points.[24] In addition, all are within the range of sample standard deviations from short-term parity reported by Frankel and MacArthur (1988) for open developed countries and are much smaller than those they report in several other categories.

The root mean square errors of the long-term Euromarket deviations are given in Column (d) of Table 1, their onshore counterparts are given in Column (d) of Table 2, and the root mean square error of the short-term deviations are given in Column (d) of Table 2. Among the long-term assets, these measures range from about 20 basis points to about 65 basis points, and they average about 30 basis points in the Euromarket and about 40 basis points in the onshore markets. These figures are only a few basis points more than the corresponding short-term measures. The short-term root mean square errors average just under 40 basis points, and they range from about 20 basis points to about 60 basis points.

Column (d) of Table l gives the bands needed to encompass 95 percent of the deviations from long-term swap parity in the Euromarket. Column (d) of Table 2 gives the comparable bands in the onshore markets, and Column (d) of Table 3 gives the short-term bands. The differences across maturities are not systematic. For Canadian, German, and U.K. assets, the bands encompassing 95 percent of the deviations are larger for long-term assets than for short-term ones, but the opposite is true of the Japanese and Swiss assets. Long-term band widths range from about 60 basis points for Canadian assets to almost 160 basis points for German assets, while the short-term band widths range from the U.K.'s band of about 70 basis points to Japan's 140 basis point band.

The remaining columns give the means of the disparities. Table 1 gives the long-term mean disparities in the Euromarket; Table 2 gives those of the onshore markets, and Table 3 gives the mean short-term disparities. All the estimated means are less than 50 basis points. The mean short-term disparities appear slightly smaller than the long-term means, but most of the standard errors are large enough to swamp those differences. Like the other disparity measures, the means are small relative to those found in countries where capital controls have been thought to be important among short-term assets.

CONCLUSIONS

This chapter provides evidence that the movement of long-term financial capital across the international bond markets of several industrialized countries is not inhibited in ways that are significant relative to the movement of short-term financial capital. This evidence comes from using a standard measure of barriers to capital mobility, covered interest parity, previously evaluated only for short-term assets, to evaluate such barriers among long-term assets. Long-term covered foreign transactions are constructed using currency and interest rate swaps. Like short-term covered transactions, these transactions leave the investor without exchange rate risk on the principal invested.

The measured deviations from long-term interest parity appear in some cases to be slightly greater than the deviations measured among short-term assets, but the differences are small. The mean absolute deviations, the mean deviations, and the measures of variability--variance, mean square error, and the size of the bands encompassing 95 percent of the covered differentials--are all consistent with this evaluation. More importantly, both the short-term and the long-term deviations from parity that are observed in the industrialized countries studied here are dwarfed by the very large deviations found in countries and time periods where capital controls have been considered to be important.

NOTES

1. That capital might be mobile across only a limited set of maturities was highlighted by the contrast between the arbitrage of short-term returns and the findings of a high correlation between countries' saving and investment. Feldstein and Horioka (1980) interpreted this as indirect evidence that "most capital is apparently not available for such arbitrage-type activity among long-term investments." While subsequent explanations of the correlation that are consistent with long-term financial capital mobility have emerged, the integration of long term bond markets has not yet been examined directly.

Short-term capital mobility, by itself, does not imply arbitrage of long-term returns. Such an implication would require either a mechanism for arbitrage across the maturity spectrum or a stable term structure relationship. Neither is supported by empirical evidence. (Shiller and McCulloch (1987) provide an extensive survey of the term structure literature.)

2. The terminology and decomposition of interest disparities due to Aliber (1973) still provides the conceptual framework for evaluating deviations from interest parity, but the appeal of transaction costs in explaining deviations has diminished as transaction costs have been more carefully measured. Clinton (1988) showed that the actual transaction cost is the smallest of the transaction costs observed in any of the markets that can be used for arbitrage. Furthermore, he showed that the existence of transaction costs is not a sufficient condition for interest disparity. In addition to the conceptual reasons for differences in returns described by Aliber, realized returns also differ as a result of variations in liquidity and taxes.

3. In the remainder of this chapter, "domestic currency" refers to the U.S. dollar, and "foreign currency" refers alternately to the Canadian dollar, the mark, the pound, the Swiss franc, or the yen.

4. Clinton (1988) examined mark, pound, yen, Canadian dollar, and French franc returns from November 1985 to May 1986. The deviations for the French franc were somewhat higher.

5. Taylor (1987) sampled covered U.S. dollar, sterling, and German mark returns every 10 minutes for three days in November, 1985.

6. The "Open Developed Countries" category includes the all the countries, except Japan, evaluated in this chapter, and it also includes the Netherlands. Japan is included in their category "Liberalizing Pacific Developed Countries, and its measured deviations are similar. "Closed Less Developed Countries" include Bahrain, Greece, Mexico, and South Africa. The sample period extends from September, 1982 to March, 1987.

7. Giavazzi and Pagano's (1985) sample period extended from September, 1982 to August 1984.

8. Giavazzi and Pagano (1985) found interest disparities in France and Italy to be largest prior to currency realignments. Between September, 1982 and the European Monetary System realignment of March, 1983, interest disparities of the same sign averaged over 900 basis points in France and over 400 basis points in Italy.

9. Measures of dispersion, rather than the mean, are emphasized for reasons discussed by Branson (1969) and outlined in Section D of this chapter.

10. An onshore-offshore comparison of same-currency returns does not require a forward market, so it could conceivably be used to assess long-term parity. However, such comparisons are easily distorted by compositional differences between the two markets.

11. Detailed statistics on such transactions are given in Bank for International Settlements (1990).

12. A currency swap is similar to the more widely traded interest rate swap in that both exchange streams of interest payments. The interest rate swap exchanges a stream of fixed dollar payments over a given time interval for a stream of floating

dollar interest payments, and its use pre-dates the widespread use of currency swaps.

13. More specifically, a currency swap exchanges a stream of non-dollar fixed payments for a stream of 6-month LIBOR (floating) payments. This contract may be combined with an interest rate swap that exchanges the LIBOR payments for a fixed rate above the U.S. Treasury bond yield. For example, to exchange five-year mark and dollar payment streams beginning July 17, 1986, an investor would have used a "cross-currency interest rate swap" which exchanged mark payments at an annual fixed rate of 5.85 percent for the floating LIBOR payments. Then, using an interest rate swap (also known as a bond swap), the stream of five-year LIBOR payments would have been exchanged for fixed dollar payments quoted in terms of a premium, then 101 basis points, over the same-maturity Treasury bond yield of 6.91 percent. In the notation of the text,

$$r_{t,\,t+s}^{sw\,*} = 5.85$$

and the equivalent fixed dollar swap payments was:

$$r_{t,\,t+s}^{sw} = 6.91 + 1.01 .$$

14. The amount of the notional swap principal may be chosen to achieve a fully hedged position.

15. Note that the swap-covered parity condition is expressed as a difference, while the short-term covered interest parity condition is expressed in terms of ratios (except as it is often approximated). This slight difference in the form of the arbitrage condition reflects the mechanics of the respective transactions. Both are one-way arbitrage conditions.

16. For the onshore government bonds, the distinction between default risk and political risk is blurred.

17. McCormick (1979) shows that the effects of mistiming errors can be large. While U.S. and Canadian yields are observed simultaneously, yields in the other markets are observed at their respective closes.

18. Actual bond yields are used for Canada, Switzerland, the United Kingdom, and the United States; while theoretical par yields are used for Germany and Japan.

Non-comparability of assets has been offered as an explanation of the negative premium measured for Eurobonds denominated in marks in particular. Even among similarly rated bonds, differences in average quality may be large enough to explain disparities of this size.

19. The sample period start dates reflect the earliest availability of reliable data. Historical swap quotes were only available weekly, and only regularly for the five-year and seven-year maturities for the markets examined here.

20. I am indebted to an anonymous referee for emphasizing the importance of this problem. Some notable aspects of the behavior of the means are summarized here.

First, the range of mean deviations observed here for *long-term* assets, -3 to 49 basis points, is nearly identical to the range of short-term means of -5 to 46 basis points reported by Frankel and MacArthur (1988) and discussed above.

Second, the mean long-term disparities are smallest, about 5 basis points, for Canadian dollar assets. German and U.K. deviations are greater in the onshore markets than in the Euromarket, their onshore deviations are between 35 and 50 basis points, while their Euromarket counterparts are about 5 to 15 basis points. For Canadian, Japanese, and Swiss assets, the differences between the onshore and offshore disparities are small and mostly insignificant.

Third, the mean deviations of Swiss franc denominated assets differ considerably between the five-year and the seven-year maturities. While the fairly large standard errors may make the difference initially uninteresting, they mask a qualitative shift in a single period: the difference between the five-year and the seven-year Swiss onshore disparities was fairly high in the early part of the sample period then declined abruptly beginning in January, 1986 when the Swiss government removed maturity limits on bonds. Before its abrupt decline in 1986, the difference between the Swiss onshore five-year and seven-year deviations from parity averaged 68 basis points.

Finally, the hypothesis that the short-term and long-term deviations are the same cannot be rejected in most of the markets. The U.K. onshore assets are the only exception. The mean swap-covered disparities in the United Kingdom of close to 50 basis points are significantly larger than the U.K.'s short-term counterpart of less than 10 basis points. However, even the U.K.'s long-term interest disparities still are within the range of deviations reported for the relatively open short-term markets discussed above.

21. The disparities are serially correlated. This may simply reflect serial correlation of transactions costs, or it may arise when deviations from parity due to political risk are persistent. Note that because the deviations from covered interest parity are known *ex ante* the ability to forecast the deviations offers no additional opportunity for arbitrage profits. Therefore, the observed serial correlation provides no additional evidence of inefficiency. Among reasonable ARMA specifications, the AR(l) is most appropriate in terms of the behavior of the deviations over the sample period and it is also the simplest. It is estimated using Hildreth-Lu, and standard errors are estimated using a linearized version of the corrected objective function.

22. The statistical significance of the mean absolute deviations is tested with a t-statistic that is modified slightly to reflect the use of absolute values. For a random variable, x, with a symmetric distribution and a mean of zero (as under the null hypothesis here), the density of $|x|$ is twice that of x. (Specifically, for the normal random variable, x, the density of $y = |x|$, call it g(y), is: $g(y) = (2/\sqrt{2\pi})\exp(-y^2/2)$, $y \rangle 0$.) So, the standard probability values must be doubled. The t-statistics are given by dividing the mean absolute deviations by the sample

standard deviations. Their (doubled) probability values are given in the table below.

Table 4

Probability Values

	3-month	5-year	7-year
Canadian Dollar	0.38	0.53	0.53
Mark	0.08	0.16	0.19
Yen	0.43	0.42	0.38
Sterling	0.49	0.23	0.14
SwissFranc	0.44	0.46	0.39

23. The range excludes France, which had much higher deviations.

24. The largest short-term standard deviations found in the onshore markets of Japan and Switzerland.

By country, the differences between the long-term and the short-term variances are statistically significant, but those differences are positive for three of the five markets and negative for the other two. The ratios of the variances, adjusted for their degrees of freedom give their F-statistics and probability values. These are presented in the table below.

Table 5

Variance Ratio: F-Statistic

	5-year	7-year
Canadian Dollar	2.37	2.53
	(.0001)	(.0001)
Mark	4.12	3.74
	(.0001)	(.0001)
Yen	0.77	0.72
	(0773)	(.0354)
Sterling	3.73	2.21
	(.0001)	(.0001)
SwissFranc	0.76	0.90
	(.0693)	(.2752)

The two other measures of variability given in the tables also appear slightly larger among long-term assets than among the corresponding short-term assets. However, they are neither uniformly nor substantially larger.

Chapter 3

Term Premia Comovement in German, Japanese, and U.S. Domestic Markets

The financial deregulation of the last two decades has removed many of the barriers that previously separated international capital markets. Ultimately, such an opening up of capital markets should allow assets to be traded as if they exist in a single market. The purpose of this investigation is to gauge the extent of that openness across the German, Japanese, and U.S. markets. Many recent studies of the integration of these capital markets have relied on tests of covered and uncovered interest parity.[1] One drawback of the interest parity approach is the narrowness of its treatment of risk. Saying nothing about the behavior of risky returns, covered interest parity is only a minimum requirement for market integration. Meanwhile, uncovered interest parity treats returns as though risk were irrelevant, so it is too strong a condition for evaluating market integration. Determining whether risky assets that are issued in potentially distinct markets are priced as though they are traded in a single market calls for an asset pricing model that embraces risk.

This study employs such a model. Specifically, it uses a latent variable version of the intertemporal capital asset pricing model.[2] Developed by Hansen and Hodrick (1983), the latent variable version of the model restricts the risky returns available to an investor to be proportional to one another. These restrictions are used here to examine the term premia of the domestic money markets of Germany, Japan, and the United States.[3,4] The proportionality restrictions should extend to these term premia if the three countries are members of a *de facto* single market.

This investigation is a natural extension of the work of Lewis (1990), Campbell and Clarida (1987), Harvey (1991), and, Campbell and Hamao (1989). The studies by Lewis and by Campbell and Clarida use the proportionality restrictions to examine the behavior of the term premia within a single market, the Euromarket. Their work is extended here to domestic markets, which have the potential to be separated by their political jurisdiction. Thus, the techniques are used here to examine the integration of international markets.

Focusing on equities, the papers by Harvey and by Campbell and Hamao also examine the behavior of asset returns across potentially distinct markets.[5] Harvey examines the stock indices of a broad range of countries. Among his many findings, he provides evidence consistent with the segmentation of the Japanese stock market from the rest of the world. While this study does not examine equity markets, it may nevertheless shed new light on Harvey's findings. If the term premia appear to arise from a single market, while Japanese equity returns do not, then the segmentation may stem from the barriers between different markets within Japan, rather than from the boundaries between countries. Campbell and Hamao also examine the predictability and comovement of Japanese and U.S. stock returns; however, they do not explicitly test for market integration.[6]

The following section briefly reviews the restrictions of the latent variable model and introduces some notation. The subsequent section describes the data and the estimation procedures. Next, the outcome of the empirical tests of the latent variable model and some related hypotheses are described. The final section concludes by interpreting these tests as evidence that the three markets are well-integrated. An appendix provides a discussion of some econometric issues and alternative formulations of the test statistics.

RETURNS IN A *DE FACTO* SINGLE MARKET

This section introduces notation and describes the restrictions implied by the latent variable version of the familiar intertemporal capital asset pricing model. Stemming from a consumer's optimal tradeoff of consumption across periods, the intertemporal capital asset pricing model restricts expected excess returns to be proportional to their covariances with the marginal rate of substitution of consumption across periods. To test the restrictions directly would require observing the marginal rate of substitution.[7]

The latent variable version of the model avoids this difficulty by reformulating the proportionality restrictions in terms of asset returns only. This reformulation is accomplished using the construct of a benchmark asset with an unobservable, *latent*, excess return, $L_{(t, t+n)}$, that is perfectly correlated with the nominal marginal rate of substitution.[8] Hansen and Hodrick show that expected excess returns should be proportional to this constructed latent variable. This investigation exploits the proportionality to examine the potentially distinct money markets of Germany, Japan and the United States. If those markets form a *de facto* single market, then their returns should all face the same proportionality restriction. In particular, the three term premia all should be proportional to the same latent variable.

Let us denote the term premium as $\mathbf{P}_{c,(t,t\,n)}$, where the first subscript gives the currency, and the next subscripts give the asset's holding period. Now, the proportionality restriction may be expressed as follows:[9]

$$\mathbf{P}_{c,(t,t+n)} = \beta_{c,t} \bullet E_t[L_{(t,t+n)}].$$

The latent variable model gains empirical content by characterizing the proportionality restrictions in terms of observable variables, x_t, known to each investor when investment decisions ares made. Expressed in terms of those variables, the term premium becomes:

$$\mathbf{P}_{c,(t,t+n)} = \beta_{c,t}(\alpha' x_t) + u_{c,t}$$

where u_t is a weighted sum of projection and expectation errors.[10] The term premia equations may be estimated directly in terms of reduced form coefficients when $\beta_{c,t}$ is a constant:[11]

(1) $$\mathbf{P}_{c,(t,t+n)} = \theta_c' x_t + u_{c,t}$$

where: $\theta_c' = \beta_c \alpha'$.

In Equation 1, the term premium in each country is expressed as a linear combination of the observable variables, where the weights, θ_c, have particular restrictions. Specifically, the coefficients of each term premium equation must be proportional to those of every other term premium equation.[12] These restrictions should hold for across international borders if capital markets are well integrated.

DATA AND ESTIMATION PROCEDURES

This section first describes the particular definition of the term premium and the data that are used. Then, it discusses a few estimation issues. The term premium is defined here as the difference between the return to holding a long-term asset and the expected return to rolling over consecutive short-term assets over the same holding period.[13] With each interval equal to one month and the holding period equal to three months, each term premium is:

$$P_{c,(t,t+3)} = E_t[(R_{c,(t,t+3)} - \prod_{i=1}^{3} R_{c,(t+i-1,t+i)}) \cdot S_{c,t}/S_{c,t+3}]$$

where $S_{c,t}$ is the foreign price of a domestic currency unit, and $R_{c,(t,t+n)}$ is an asset's gross n-period return.

In this investigation, the U.S. dollar is treated as the domestic currency. The U.S. and Japanese returns are taken from annualized yields on thirty-day and ninety-day certificates of deposit within each of the two countries. German yields are from one-month and three-month German interbank loans. Equation 1 is estimated for each country using these definitions and a common set of information variables.

The power of a test to reject the proportionality restrictions imposed by the latent variable version of the asset pricing model (or any of the stronger restrictions, such as those of the expectations hypothesis) depends on the predictive value of the information variables used in explaining the term premia. So, the information variables in the term premia equations should be chosen for their predictive ability.

Existing studies have found two types of interest rate spreads, both known *ex ante*, to be particularly good predictors of the term premium: term *spreads* and interest rate spreads across currencies.[14] Stock and Watson (1990) and Estrella and Hardouvelis (1989) show that the U.S. term spread, besides being a good predictor of the premium, is also a good indicator of real economic activity in the United States. Their results regarding real activity are important here since the predictions of a latent variable version of the intertemporal capital asset pricing model ultimately rely on the comovement of asset prices with real variables. Campbell and Clarida, Hodrick and Srivastava (1984) and Lewis show that nominal interest rate differences across currencies help to predict some excess Eurocurrency returns.[15]

Both the term spread and the cross-country interest rate spreads are used here as information variables. They include the U.S. term spread and the interest rate spreads between the United States and Germany and between the United States and Japan.[16] More specifically, they are: the difference between the ninety-day and thirty-day U.S. yields ($R_{us(t, t+3)}$ - $R_{us(t, t+1)}$), the difference between the yield on the U.S. ninety-day certificate of deposit and on the German three-month interbank rate ($R_{us(t, t+3)}$ - $R_{ge(t, t+3)}$), and the difference between the yields on the U.S. and on the Japanese nintey-day certificates of deposit ($R_{us(t, t+3)}$ - $R_{ja(t, t+3)}$).

The observations are drawn weekly. This sampling results in the overlapping observations structure and the corresponding moving average error process described by Hansen and Hodrick (1980).[17] Their procedure for consistent estimation of the variance-covariance matrix addresses the serial correlation, and a modified version that allows for conditional heteroskedasticity is used here.[18] The sample period extends from October, 1986 to July, 1988, a period encompassing the stock market crash of October 1987.

ESTIMATES AND HYPOTHESIS TESTS

This section first describes the estimates of the coefficients of the unrestricted versions of the term premium equation (Equation 1). Next, it discusses the outcome of the tests of the latent variable model and the more restrictive hypotheses that it nests. Finally, it interprets the findings in the context of related studies.

Estimates of the unrestricted versions of Equation 1 are given in Table 6. The first column gives the U.S. estimates, their standard errors, and the equation's R^2. The next two columns give the corresponding statistics for Germany and for Japan. In each country, the four coefficients are jointly statistically significant, and a third of the coefficients are individually significant. The difference between the U.S. and German three-month returns is significant in the German term premium equation, and the difference between the U.S. and Japanese three-month rates is significant in the U.S. term premium equation. In the Japanese term premium equation, only the constant is individually significant. The coefficients on the U.S. term spread are positive in all three term premium equations, but nowhere is it individually significant. The goodness of fit statistic is roughly 40 percent in each equation.

Table 7 reports the test statistic for the hypothesis that the term premia in the three countries equal one another, and it gives the contemporaneous correlations of the term premia. As shown in the top panel of the table, it is easy to reject the hypothesis that the coefficients are the same in the three eqations. Note that this rejection of the equality of the three term premia is not necessarily indicative of segmented markets. Even in a single market, equality of excess returns is expected only when their

Table 6

Unrestricted Term Premia Estimates

$$P_{c,(t,t+3)} = (R_{c,(t,t+3)} - \prod_{i=1}^{3} R_{c,(t+i-1,t+i)}) \cdot \frac{S_{c,t}}{S_{c,(t+3)}} =$$

$$\theta_{c,1} + \theta_{c,2}(R_{us,(t,t+3)} - R_{us,(t,t+1)}) +$$

$$\theta_{c,3}(R_{us,(t,t+3)} - R_{ge,(t,t+3)}) +$$

$$\theta_{c,4}(R_{us,(t,t+3)} - R_{ja,(t,t+3)}) + v_{c,t}$$

	Market		
Coefficients	United States	Germany	Japan
θ_1	-.570*	.146	.182*
s.e.(θ_1)	(.167)	(.237)	(.091)
θ_2	.308	.639	.305
s.e.(θ_2)	(.416)	(.416)	(.224)
θ_3	-.032	-.299*	.002
s.e.(θ_3)	(.133)	(.134)	(.042)
θ_4	.294*	.299	-.055
s.e.(θ_4)	(.129)	(.187)	(.061)
R^2	.437	.397	.442

Explanatory Notes:

a. Notation: **S** is the exchange rate, **R** is the interbank rate. Subscripts index currency and time period.

b. The sample period extends from October 22, 1986 to July 27, 1988.

c. Standard error estimates are heteroskedastic and moving-average consistent.

d. An asterisk indicates a coefficient statistically different from zero at a 95 percent confidence level.

Table 7

Term Premia Comovement

$$P_{c,(t,t+3)} = \left(R_{c,(t,t+3)} - \prod_{i=1}^{3} R_{c,(t+i-1,t+i)}\right) \cdot \frac{S_{c,t}}{S_{c,(t+3)}} =$$

$$\theta_{c,1} + \theta_{c,2}\,(R_{us,(t,t+3)} - R_{us,(t,t+1)}) +$$

$$\theta_{c,3}\,(R_{us,(t,t+3)} - R_{ge,(t,t+3)}) +$$

$$\theta_{c,4}\,(R_{us,(t,t+3)} - R_{ja,(t,t+3)}) + v_{c,t}$$

H_0: $\theta_{us} = \theta_{ge} = \theta_{ja}$	$\chi^2(8)$	28.72
	prob	.999

Contemporaneous Correlations

	United States	Germany	Japan
United States	1.0	0.53	0.43
Germany		1.00	0.51
Japan			1.00

Explanatory Notes:

a. Notation: **S** is the exchange rate, **R** is the interbank rate. Subscripts index currency and time period.
b. The sample period extends from October 22, 1986 to July 27, 1988.
c. Standard error estimates are heteroskedastic and moving-average consistent.
d. An asterisk indicates a coefficient statistically different from zero at a 95 percent confidence level.

riskiness is unimportant or identical. As shown in the bottom panel, the correlations are close to one-half. The test of the hypothesis that the equation coefficients are identical is easilly rejected.

Additional Statistics are given in Tables 8 and 9. The statistic for testing the restrictions of the latent variable model is given in the top panel of Table 8. It is a χ^2 statistic constructed as a Wald test using the unrestricted parameter estimates given in Table 6. The test statistics are based on the unrestricted model instead of the restricted model because of some undesirable small sample properties inherent in the usual constrained estimation procedures.[19] Because different formulations of the Wald statistic result in different test statistics, a number of different formulations are presented in the appendix, as are the generalized method of moments constrained estimates and test statistic. As the χ^2 statistic shows, the restrictions that the coefficients in the term premium equations are proportional to one another cannot be rejected at any standard significance level.

Because the term premia are cast in a single currency, they reflect exchange rate risk as well as interest rate risk. The latent variable model nests the most common hypotheses regarding these two risky elements: the expectations hypothesis of the term structure of interest rates, and the hypothesis of uncovered interest rate parity.[20] Both hypotheses narrowly constrain an expected risky return to equal a nominally risk-free one.[21] Slightly less restrictive variants allow for non-zero constant risk premia.

Since so much theoretical work continues to rely on these hypotheses, their restrictions also are tested explicitly despite their frequent rejection elsewhere.[22] The test statistics for these hypotheses are given in the bottom panel of Table 8. As nested within the latent variable model, the two hypotheses together imply that all the coefficients in each country equal zero. These constraints are strongly rejected for the three countries together and individually.

Table 8
Hypothesis Tests

$$P_{c,(t,t+3)} = (R_{c,(t,t+3)} - \prod_{i=1}^{3} R_{c,(t+i-1,t+i)}) \cdot \frac{S_{c,t}}{S_{c,(t+3)}} =$$

$$\theta_{c,1} + \theta_{c,2}(R_{us,(t,t+3)} - R_{us,(t,t+1)}) +$$

$$\theta_{c,3}(R_{us,(t,t+3)} - R_{ge,(t,t+3)}) +$$

$$\theta_{c,4}(R_{us,(t,t+3)} - R_{ja,(t,t+3)}) + v_{c,t}$$

Proportional Term Premia

H_o: $(\theta_{a,i} \cdot \theta_{k,1}) - (\theta_{a,1} \cdot \theta_{k,i}) = 0$

(i = 2 to 4; k = United States, Germany)

$\chi^2(6)$	5.66
probability	0.54

The Pure Expectations Hypothesis

H_o: $\theta_{c,i} = 0$, i = 1 to 4

	U.S. $\chi^2(4)$	Germany $\chi^2(4)$	Japan $\chi^2(4)$	Combined $\chi^2(12)$
	18.35	9.63	59.04	87.01
probabilty	0.99	0.95	.99	.99

Explanatory Notes:

a. Notation: **S** is the exchange rate, **R** is the interbank rate. Subscripts index currency and time period.
b. The sample period extends from October 22, 1986 to July 27, 1988.
c. Standard error estimates are heteroskedastic and moving-average consistent.
d. An asterisk indicates a coefficient statistically different from zero at a 95 percent confidence level.

Table 9

Constant Risk Premium

$$P_{c,(t,t+3)} = \left(R_{c,(t,t+3)} - \prod_{i=1}^{3} R_{c,(t+i-1,t+i)}\right) \cdot \frac{S_{c,t}}{S_{c,(t+3)}} =$$

$$\theta_{c,1} + \theta_{c,2}\left(R_{us,(t,t+3)} - R_{us,(t,t+1)}\right) +$$

$$\theta_{c,3}\left(R_{us,(t,t+3)} - R_{ge,(t,t+3)}\right) +$$

$$\theta_{c,4}\left(R_{us,(t,t+3)} - R_{ja,(t,t+3)}\right) + v_{c,t}$$

$$H_o: \quad \theta_{c,i} = 0$$

$$i = 2 \text{ to } 4$$

	U.S. $\chi^2(3)$	Germany $\chi^2(3)$	Japan $\chi^2(3)$	Combined $\chi^2(9)$
test statistic	16.83	6.64	2.60	26.07
probability	0.99	0.92	0.54	0.99

Explanatory Notes:

a. Notation: **S** is the exchange rate, **R** is the interbank rate. Subscripts index currency and time period.
b. The sample period extends from October 22, 1986 to July 27, 1988.
c. Standard error estimates are heteroskedastic and moving-average consistent.
d. An asterisk indicates a coefficient statistically different from zero at a 95 percent confidence level.

The somewhat less restrictive hypothesis of constant exchange risk and term premia implies that for each country all the coefficients other than the constant equal zero. As shown in the Table 9, this hypothesis is rejected at standard confidence levels for the three countries together and individually for the United States and Germany, though not for Japan. The rejection of these narrow restrictions even within individual markets, rather than evincing barriers to capital mobility, underscores the importance of an adequate consideration of risk in assessing market integration. In the context of the latent variable version of the intertemporal capital asset pricing model, the empirical results suggests a high degree of comovement of the term premia across the onshore markets of the United States, Germany, and Japan. From the point of view of a single investor, the returns appear to behave as if the assets are traded in a single market.

The evidence of term premia comovement across these markets extends to onshore markets the work of Campbell and Clarida, who find that differences in the currency of denomination do not appear to segment the Euromarket.[23,24] This evidence, consistent with open money markets, also suggests that Harvey's finding of Japanese stock market segmentation may arise from barriers within Japan, rather than from barriers between countries. These results also extend to risky assets the findings of market integration reported by those examining covered interest parity.[25] This study's results suggest that in Germany, Japan, and the United States, political and geographic differences are not important enough to segment this larger set of markets.

CONCLUSIONS

Repeated rejections of models that equate risky and riskless returns highlight the importance of an adequate treatment of risk in any broad assessment of the integration of financial markets. The latent variable version of the intertemporal capital asset pricing model has been used to describe the behavior of risky returns within the Euromarket, other single markets, and equity markets. This investigation extends the application of the latent variable framework. Using the term premia, it focuses on the integration of markets across the political jurisdictions that might separate them. That is, the study assesses whether these risky assets in potentially distinct markets are priced similarly and subject to the same shocks. The viewpoint of an individual investor is adopted, and the restrictions of the latent variable model are tested for the term premia in German, Japanese, and U.S. onshore markets. The latent variable model restricts risky returns to move in constant proportion to one another. The restrictions of the model are not rejected here. This result is suggestive of openness across the money markets of Germany, Japan, and the United States.

NOTES

1. Covered interest parity equates a domestic-currency return with a covered foreign-currency return, so it includes no exchange rate risk. Uncovered interest parity equates a nominally riskless domestic-currency return with an expected foreign-currency return that is risky in terms of its final value in domestic currency. By equating a riskless domestic-currency return with a risky foreign-currency return, uncovered interest parity assumes that exchange rate risk is irrelevant in the sense that it is not priced. As would be expected, uncovered interest parity is often rejected in markets where covered interest parity appears to hold.

2. The latent variable version of the intertemporal capital asset pricing model provides a fairly general approach to modeling returns that, as discussed in the second section of this chapter, does not face the same difficulties as direct estimation of the capital asset pricing model.

3. The importance of the term structure of interest rates in the transmission of independent macroeconomic policies makes the question of international integration of capital markets particularly germane for the term structure. Turnovsky (1989) provides a detailed discussion of the relationship between macroeconomic policies and the term structure.

4. In this study, the term premia are expressed in a single currency so that they may be compared from the viewpoint of an individual investor.

5. Campbell (1987) also uses the latent variable version of the intertemporal capital asset pricing model to examine asset returns, but he restricts his investigation to U.S. assets. Campbell and Hamao also examine bond yields.

6. In emphasizing the predictability of returns, Campbell and Hamao do not attempt to measure risky returns from the viewpoint of a single investor. Instead, they examine the predictability and comovement of Japanese and U.S. stock returns denominated in the two different currencies, so the proportionality restrictions need

not hold even with wholly open markets.

7. Like most measures of real economic activity, observations of consumption are typically available infrequently and measured imprecisely relative to observations of asset prices.

8. The benchmark asset may be a portfolio, and there may be more than one latent variable. Campbell uses three latent variables to characterize various U.S. assets in the U.S. market.

9. Although a foreign term premium is a *difference* between expected excess returns, the proportionality restrictions still apply, and:

$$\beta_{c,t} = cov_t[(R_{c,(t,t+n)} - \prod_{i=1}^{n} R_{c,(t+i-1,t+i)}) \cdot S_{c,t}/S_{c,t+n} , L_{(t,t+n)}] \;/\; var_t[L_{(t,t+n)}]$$

where: $R_{c,(t,t+n)}$ is the gross return; and, $S_{c,t}$ is the foreign currency price of a domestic currency unit.

10. This expression comes from linearly projecting the latent variable onto the observable variables. If expectations are formed rationally, then:

$$P_{c,(t,t+n)} = \beta_{c,t} E_t(L_{(t,t+n)}) + v_{c,t},$$

where $E_t(v_{c,t}) = 0$, and $L_{(t,t+n)} = \alpha' x_t + e_t$. So:

$$u_{c,t} = \beta_{c,t} e_t + v_{c,t}.$$

11. More generally, this estimation requires only that the ratios of the betas $(\beta_{i,t}/\beta_{j,t})$ be constant.

12. For any two countries, i and j, the coefficients are a scalar multiple of each other: $\theta_i = k\theta_j$, where $k = \beta_i/\beta_j$. For three countries and four information variables, this provides six over-identifying restrictions.

13. Shiller and McCulloch (1986) present simple relationships between numerous empirical formulations of the expectations hypothesis, including the roll-over term premium described here. Campbell, Shiller and Shoenholtz (1983) derive a discrete-time linearized version with which several theoretical formulations are

consistent.

14. The term spread is the difference between the (known) long-term nominal return and the (known) initial short-term nominal return.

15. Given covered interest parity, the differences in the Eurodeposit rates approximate the forward exchange premia.

16. Given covered interest parity, the differences in the Eurodeposit rates approximate the forward exchange premia.

17. In the case of the domestic asset, agents' expectation errors remain unresolved for 2 months, at which time $R_{(t+2,\ t+3)}$ becomes known; so, weekly sampling results in an eighth order moving average error process. For foreign assets, the uncertainty remains until the exchange rate uncertainty is resolved when the asset matures in 3 months, so weekly sampling results in a thirteenth order moving average error.

18. Hodrick and Srivastava (1984) and Giovannini and Jorion (1987) both find evidence of conditional heteroskedasticity of asset returns. The heteroskedastic version of Hansen and Hodrick's (1980) variance-covariance estimator used here is

$$(X'X)^{-1}\ X'WX(X'X)^{-1},$$

where X is the matrix of observed information variables and W is formed from consistent error estimates, $\hat{u}$. The (m,n)th element of W (where m and n index the time period) equals $\hat{u}_m\ \hat{u}_n g_{m,n}$, when $(|m-n|+l)$ is less than the order of the moving average lag, k, and equals zero otherwise. The weight, $g_{m,n}$, is chosen by Newey and West (1985) to equal $[1-|m-n|/(k+l)]$.

19. The generalized method of moments estimators are extremely sensitive to starting values in this case; and maximum likelihood convergence is particularly difficult because of the error structure. For a discussion of the small sample properties of generalized method of moments parameter estimates see Chapter 4.

20. The expectations hypothesis equates the expected return to a series of short-term assets with a known long-term return, and uncovered interest parity equates the expected risky return to a foreign-currency denominated asset with a known home-currency return. In the framework of intertemporal asset pricing models, each hypothesis requires that the covariance between each risky return and the marginal rate of substitution of consumption is zero.

21. The expectations hypothesis of the term structure equates the expected return to the risky strategy of rolling over consecutive returns with the known nominal return over the entire period,

$$E_t \left(R_{t,t+3} - \prod_{i=1}^{3} R_{t+i-1,t+i}\right) = 0$$

Uncovered interest parity equates the expected risky foreign return with the known domestic return:

$$E_t \left(R_{t,t+3} - R_{c,(t,t+3)} \cdot S_t/S_{t+3}\right) = 0$$

22. Shiller and McCulloch (1986) survey tests of the expectations theory of the term structure, and Hodrick (1987) surveys tests of the hypothesis that forward exchange rates are unbiased predictors of future spot rates. Both report frequent rejections.

23. Both the evidence presented here and the results of Campbell and Clarida contrast with the rejections of the latent variable model for the short holding periods examined by Giovannini and Jorion (1987) and Hodrick and Srivastava. However, Lewis notes that rejection occurs infrequently in the Euromarket when the holding period exceeds one month. Since comparable onshore returns at very short maturities were not available, it was not possible to examine the sensitivity of the onshore results to maturity.

24. Outside the Euromarket, the latent variable model has been used by Campbell o examine a wide set of U.S. assets and by Campbell and Hamao in evaluating the comovement of U.S. and

Japanese stock returns. Both studies reject the single latent variable model, but neither implies segmented international capital markets. Campbell includes only U.S. assets and suggests his rejection may be due to the long sample period (20 years) during which very slow changes in betas may become relevant. Campbell and Hamao, emphasizing the predictability of returns, do not attempt to measure risky returns from the viewpoint of a single investor. Instead, they examine the predictability and comovement of Japanese and U.S. stock returns denominated in the two different currencies, so the proportionality restrictions need not hold even in a wholly open market.

25. See, for example, Frankel (1991), Kasman and Pigott (1988), Frankel, Phillips, and Chinn (forthcoming), and Popper (1993).

Appendix to Chapter 3
Formulation of the Wald Statistic

This appendix discusses the construction of the Wald statistic used to test the latent variable model described in Chapter 3. The restrictions of the latent variable model are nonlinear, and they may be expressed in many algebraically equivalent ways. Gregory and Veall (1985) show that the Wald statistics arising from algebraically equivalent formulations of nonlinear hypotheses are not numerically the same, despite their large sample equivalence.[1] Since the testable implications of the latent variable model are fundamentally nonlinear, their work implies that tests of the model must be sensitive to the formulation of the hypothesis. Yet, to test the model, a choice of must be made regarding the appropriate formulation. Here, guidance in choosing a formulation is taken from the scalar results of both simulations by Gregory and Veall and the analytical work of Phillips and Park (1988). In addition, Monte Carlo simulations are used. Finally, the model is tested using generalized method of moments.

The latent variable model, itself, restricts the parameters to be inversely related.[2] The hypothesis may be written in many ways. Here we consider two specific formulations of the hypothesis. For convenience, we call the first the multiplicative formulation, and we call the second the proportionate formulation. These may be written as follows:

Multiplicative Formulation:

$$P_{c,(t,t+n)} - {}_j\beta\, \alpha' x_t = 0$$

Proportionate Formulation:

$$\frac{P_{c,(t,t+n)}}{{}_j\beta} - \alpha' x_t = 0.$$

While the two formulations are algebraically equivalent, they are nonlinear reparameterizations of each other and yield numerically different Wald statistics.

Table 10 and Table 11 give the χ^2 statistics calculated from the multiplicative formulation and from the proportionate formulation. Because the choice of the country for normalization is also arbitrary, a separate statistic is given for each normalization. The Wald statistics that have been constructed using the multiplicative formulation are given in Table 6. Consistent with the results presented in Chapter 3, the latent variable model cannot be rejected in any of the multiplicative formulations.

Tests of the model using the proportionate formulation are given in Table 10. In clear contrast to the results obtained using the multiplicative formulation, the single-beta latent variable model is now rejected at all standard significance levels.

Table 10

Multiplicative Hypothesis Formulation

$$P_{c,(t,t+3)} = (R_{c,(t,t+3)} - \prod_{i=1}^{3} R_{c,(t+i-1,t+i)}) \cdot \frac{S_{c,t}}{S_{c,(t+3)}} =$$

$$\theta_{c,1} + \theta_{c,2}(R_{us,(t,t+3)} - R_{us,(t,t+1)}) + \theta_{c,3}(R_{us,(t,t+3)} - R_{ge,(t,t+3)}) + \theta_{c,4}(R_{us,(t,t+3)} - R_{ja,(t,t+3)}) + v_{c,t}$$

$$H_o: \quad (\theta_{c,i} \cdot \theta_{k,1}) - (\theta_{c,1} \cdot \theta_{k,i}) = 0 \qquad i = 2 \text{ to } 4$$

	c = Japan k = U.S., Germany	c = Germany k = U.S., Japan	c = U.S. k = Japan, Germany
$\chi^2(6)$	5.66	5.65	9.40
probability	0.54	0.54	0.85

Explanatory Notes:

a. Notation: **S** is the exchange rate, **R** is the interbank rate. Subscripts index currency and time period.
b. The sample period extends from October 22, 1986 to July 27, 1988.
c. Standard error estimates are heteroskedastic and moving-average consistent.
d. An asterisk indicates a coefficient statistically different from zero at a 95 percent confidence level.

Table 11

Proportionate Hypothesis Formulation

$$P_{c,(t,t+3)} = (R_{c,(t,t+3)} - \prod_{t=1}^{3} R_{c,(t+i-1,t+i)}) \cdot \frac{S_{c,t}}{S_{c,(t+3)}} =$$

$$\theta_{c,1} + \theta_{c,2} (R_{us,(t,t+3)} - R_{us,(t,t+1)}) +$$

$$\theta_{c,3} (R_{us,(t,t+3)} - R_{ge,(t,t+3)}) +$$

$$\theta_{c,4} (R_{us,(t,t+3)} - R_{ja,(t,t+3)}) + v_{c,t}$$

$$H_o: \quad \theta_{k,i} - \theta_{k,1} \cdot (\theta_{c,i}/\theta_{c,1}) = 0 \qquad i = 2 \text{ to } 4$$

	c = Japan k = U.S., Germany	c = Germany k = U.S., Japan	c = U.S. k = Japan,
Germany			
$\chi^2(6)$	39.39	22.94	30.77
probability	0.99	0.99	0.99

Explanatory Notes:

a. Notation: **S** is the exchange rate, **R** is the interbank rate. Subscripts index currency and time period.

b. The sample period extends from October 22, 1986 to July 27, 1988.

c. Standard error estimates are heteroskedastic and moving-average consistent.

d. An asterisk indicates a coefficient statistically different from zero at a 95 percent confidence level.

The intuition of Gregory and Veall lends insight into why these results might differ so sharply and some guidance regarding the choice of parameterization. They point out that approximations of inverse functions that rely on derivatives might be very poor when the value of the function is close to zero. Then then suggest that the multiplicative alternative should be prefered in that case. Here, many of the coefficient estimates in the term premia equations are indeed small.[3]

A Monte Carlo experiment also supports the choice of the multiplicative formulation of the hypothesis. The unrestricted parameter estimates given in Table 6 are used to construct the Wald statistics for both formulations with the latent variable model taken as true. These include the estimated coefficients in the U.S. term premium equation and the estimated constants in the term premium equations for Germany and Japan.

Table 11 gives the results of this experiment using 1000 draws of normal random variables. The first column gives the number of rejections using the multiplicative formulation; and the second column gives the number of rejections using the proportionate formulation. At the 5 percent confidence level, the Wald statistic constructed from the multiplicative formulation rejected the latent variable model (true by construction) in about 3 percent of the draws. In contrast, the proportionate formulation rejected the model in nearly 85 percent of the draws. At the 50 percent confidence level, the multiplicative formulation rejected the model in just over 60 percent of the draws, while the proportional formulation rejected the model in over 95 percent.

By illustrating that the proportionate formulation rejects far too often, the Monte Carlo experiment provides some support the formulation choice of Chapter 3. In addition, the experiment demonstrates in a multivariate setting the dramatic effect of highly non-linear reparameterizations, and the Wald's poor finite sample properties when values close to zero appear in the denominator of the hypothesis formulation.

Table 12

Monte Carlo Simulations of Wald Statistics Using Alternative Parameterizations

$$P_{c,(t,t+3)} = (R_{c,(t,t+3)} - \prod_{i=1}^{3} R_{c,(t+i-1,t+i)}) \cdot \frac{S_{c,t}}{S_{c,(t+3)}} =$$

$$\theta_{c,1} + \theta_{c,2} (R_{us,(t,t+3)} - R_{us,(t,t+1)}) +$$

$$\theta_{c,3} (R_{us,(t,t+3)} - R_{ge,(t,t+3)}) +$$

$$\theta_{c,4} (R_{us,(t,t+3)} - R_{ja,(t,t+3)}) + v_{c,t}$$

	Number of Rejections from 1000 Trials	
	Multiplicative Formulation	Proportionate Formulation
Confidence Level	H_o: $(\theta_{c,i} \cdot \theta_{us,1}) - (\theta_{c,1} \cdot \theta_{us,i}) = 0$	H_o $\theta_{c,i} - \theta_{c,1} \cdot (\theta_{us,i}/\theta_{us,1}) = 0$
95 percent	29	845
90 percent	72	881
75 percent	263	926
50 percent	627	957
25 percent	907	982

Table 13
Generalized Method of Moments Estimates

Orthogonality Conditions: $(P_t - \alpha\beta' x_t) \otimes x_t = (0\ 0 \ldots 0)$

Parameter Estimates

U.S. Coefficients

Constant	α_1	-0.059
Term Spread	α_2	0.358
Mark Spread	α_3	-0.058
Yen Spread	α_4	0.104

Proportionality Factors
(Normalization: $\beta_{us} = 1$)

Germany	β_{ge}	1.0027
Japan	β_{ja}	1.169

Test of the Latent Variable Model's Restrictions

$\chi^2(6)$	6.162
probability	0.595

Explanatory Notes:

a. Notation: $P_t \equiv$ German, Japanese, and U.S. term premia, $x_t \equiv$ a vector of the information variables: the term spread and 3-month interest rate spreads between the United States and Germany and between the United States and Japan.

b. The overidentifying restrictions implicit in the orthogonality conditions are: $\theta' = \alpha\beta'$.

c. This estimation used a modified version of the useful GAUSS generalized method of moments procedure written by Lars P. Hansen, John C. Heaton, and Masao Ogaki, under NSF Grant No. SES-8512371.

d. Starting values are taken from the estimates given in Table 6 of the unrestricted U.S. term premium equation and the constants in the German and Japanese term premia equations.

Finally, Table 13 provides the generalized method of moments estimates of the latent variable model. The starting values for the generalized method of moments estimation are taken from the unrestricted estimates of Table 6. The top panel of the table gives the parameter estimates for the U.S. term premia equation; the middle panel of the table gives the estimated proportionality factors; and the bottom panel of the table gives the test of the latent variable hypothesis. As shown, the latent variable model of the term premia is not rejected at any standard level of significance. Thus, the generalized method of moments statistic also is consistent with the empirical results reported above.

NOTES TO APPENDIX

1. The problem stems from the fact that the asymptotic properties of the Wald statistic rely on a Taylor approximation of the null hypothesis. The approximation can be a poor one when the hypothesis or its reparameterization is extremely nonlinear.

2. Gregory and Veall's classic example is the hypothesis that one parameter is the inverse of another; that is H_0: a = l/b. This may be written either as H_0: a - l/b = 0, or as H_0: ab - 1 = 0. The two formulations yield distinct tests statistics. Gregory and Veall provide Monte Carlo evidence showing that the difference can be large and that it depends on the parameter values. The analytical work of Phillips and Park and of Lafontaine and White amplifies the point.

3. Phillips and Park analytically compare alternative parameterizations similar to those of Gregory and Veall by evaluating the higher order terms of the Taylor approximations. While their work has not been extended to multivariate cases, it reinforces the conclusions of Gregory and Veall.

Chapter 4

Formulating Non-linear Moment Conditions for Generalized Method of Moments Estimators

Ever since Robert Lucas (1976) demonstrated the importance of characterizing economic behavior in terms of parameters that are invariant to policy interventions, many economists have attempted to improve the estimates of such underlying parameters. Prominent among the advances in estimation techniques is the generalized method of moments procedure of Hansen (1982) and Hansen and Singleton (1982). The Generalized method of moments procedure is attractive because it requires only very weak distributional and structural assumptions, and it is commonly used to estimate the parameters of non-linear rational expectations models. The Generalized method of moments estimates are obtained by minimizing a function of sample deviations from a model's implied restrictions.

This paper illustrates the sensitivity of the resulting estimates to the way in which the model's restrictions are expressed.

The choice of how to formulate a model's restrictions is often arbitrary. For example, economic theory may establish that a consumer's marginal rate of substitution is equal to a relative price; but, theory often does not dictate whether that equality is expressed better by noting that the difference between the two variables should equal zero, or, alternatively, that their ratio should equal one. These seemingly trivial distinctions can involve transforming the hypothesized conditions in ways that are non-linear in terms of the parameters of interest. Consequently, they can alter the minimization problem solved in the Generalized method of moments procedure. In that case, alternative formulations yield alternative parameter estimates. This parameter sensitivity is not important in purely linear problems or when theory makes the choice of formulation clear. However, the strength of Generalized method of moments stems from its usefulness in problems that are both highly non-linear and lacking in theoretical restrictions. Thus, parameter sensitivity is important in many generalized method of moments applications.

This paper uses a very simple data generating process to illustrate the parameter sensitivity. First, the general problem is briefly described. Then, a Monte Carlo experiment is used to compare alternative parameter estimates arising in the specific non-linear rational expectations model examined by Hansen and Singleton, the representative consumer model.

SENSITIVITY TO THE FORMULATION OF THE MOMENT CONDITIONS.

Consider a model with r restrictions (moment conditions) that may be formulated in various ways. Two of the possible formulations may be written so that one is a simple transformation of the other.

Parameterization 1: $E_t [f (x_t, \theta)] = 0$

Parameterization 2: $E_t [f_a(x_t, \theta)] = 0$

where: $f_a(x_t, \theta) = R(\theta) f(x_t, \theta)$.

Here, both $f(x_t, \theta)$ and $f_a(x_t, \theta)$ are functions of a stationary observable process (x_t) and a vector of *k* parameters (θ); and E_t denotes an expectation conditioned on information available at period t.[1] For simplicity, let $R(\theta)$ be a scalar that is constant over time.[2]

Since the moment conditions cannot all be satisfied in any finite sample when their number exceeds the number of parameters being estimated, the generalized method of moments procedure weights the hypothesized moment conditions and makes the weighted sample deviations from those conditions small. Specifically, the generalized method of moments estimators that correspond to the above two alternative parameterizations minimize the following two expressions: $(g_T' W_g g_T)$ and $(g_{aT}' W_{ga} g_{aT})$, where g_T and g_{aT} are the vectors of the corresponding sample moments,

$$g_T = \frac{1}{T}\sum_{t=1}^{T} f(x_t, \theta_T)$$

$$g_{aT} = R(\theta_T)\, g_T ,$$

and W_g and W_{ga} are weighting matrices.[3]

Since the minimization problems differ, the Generalized method of moments estimates (θ_{gmm} and $\theta_{a, gmm}$) resulting from the two parameterizations solve different sets of first order conditions. Denoting these conditions as FOC 1 and FOC 2, they can be written as follows:

FOC 1: $(\partial g_T / \partial \theta)' W_g \, g_T = 0$

FOC 2: $(\partial g_{aT} / \partial \theta)' W_{ga} \, g_{aT} = 0.$

The same estimate does not in general satisfy both sets of first-order conditions. To compare the first order conditions, it is useful to expand the terms of FOC 2, to give FOC 2':[4]

FOC 2': $$\frac{\partial g_T'}{\partial \theta} W_g g_T + \left[\frac{\partial R(\theta)}{\partial \theta} \cdot \frac{R(\theta)}{R(\theta_o)^2} \right] g_T' W_g g_T = 0.$$

The first term in FOC 2′ is simply the expression set equal to zero in FOC 1.

Term 1: $$\left(\frac{\partial g_T'}{\partial \theta} W_g g_T\right) = 0$$

When the two parameter estimates are identical, this term equals zero. The second term of FOC 2′ must also equal zero at the same parameter value in order to satisfy both sets of first order conditions.

$$\text{Term 2:} \qquad \frac{\partial R(\theta)}{\partial \theta} \cdot \frac{R(\theta)}{R(\theta_o)^2} \cdot g_T' W_g g_T,$$

Only under two circumstances will this second term equal zero at the same parameter value. The term will equal zero if the reparameterization is a linear one, so that:

$$\frac{\partial R(\theta)}{\partial \theta} = 0 .$$

This implies that the generalized method of moments estimator is invariant to *linear* transformations of the moment conditions.

Second, it will equal zero if $g_T' W_g g_T$ equals zero. This last expression is the objective function minimized in the first parameterization, and it will equal zero only if the population moment conditions are exactly satisfied in the sample. So, uniqueness of the generalized method of moments estimator is limited to cases where alternative non-linear reparameterizations are excluded, or where the hypothesized moment conditions are exactly satisfied in the sample (in which case the generalized method of moments weights are irrelevant). Otherwise, the generalized method of moments estimator is sensitive to the specific formulation chosen to express the moment conditions. Since empirical models often suggest several alternative non-linear reparameterizations, this parameter sensitivity can be important.

An Example: The Representative Consumer

This section uses a Monte Carlo experiment to examine a particular example of parameter sensitivity. In their seminal paper, Hansen and Singleton demonstrate the technique of generalized method of moments by using the Euler conditions of a representative consumer to estimate the consumer's degree of risk aversion, α, and discount factor, β. This section combines the same Euler conditions with simulated data from a very simple data generating process to examine generalized method of moments estimators constructed from two specific formulations of those Euler conditions. In repeated samples, the two formulations yield noticeably different estimates.

Hansen and Singleton consider a consumer with constant relative risk averse preferences:

$$U(C_t) = \frac{C_t^{1+\alpha}}{1+\alpha},$$

where C_t denotes real consumption at period t. Maximizing this consumer's discounted expected utility subject to the usual intertemporal budget constraint gives the following Euler condition:

$$\beta E_t[(\frac{C_{t+1}}{C_t})^{\alpha} R_{t+1}] = 1,$$

where R_t denotes a one-period real return.

Generalized method of moments is used to estimate the unknown parameters by rewriting the above equation in terms of a disturbance whose conditional expectation is zero. Such a disturbance may be formulated in many ways. Here, we consider two such formulations, which we denote as $h_1(x_t, \theta)$ and $h_2(x_t, \theta)$. The corresponding moment conditions are as follows:

$$E_t[h_1(x_{t+1},\theta)] = E_t[\beta(\frac{C_{t+1}}{C_t})^{\alpha} R_{t+1} - 1] = 0$$

$$E_t[h_2(x_{t+1},\theta)] = E_t[\ (\frac{C_{t+1}}{C_t})^{\alpha} R_{t+1} - \frac{1}{\beta}] = 0$$

where:[5]

$$\theta = (\beta,\alpha)'$$

$$x_{t+n} = (\frac{C_{t+n}}{C_t}, R_{t+n}).$$

Without additional economic theory or information regarding the distribution of these disturbances, the choice between the two formulations is arbitrary.

Either formulation may be used to construct a family of moment conditions using a set of instruments, z_{t+1}, known at period t, as follows:

$$E[\ h_i\,(x_{t+1}, \theta) \otimes z_t\,] = 0,$$

where i = 1, 2. The generalized method of moments estimators minimize corresponding functions of the sample moment conditions, as given below.

$$J_{iT}(\theta) = g_{iT}(\theta)' W_{iT}\, g_{iT}(\theta)$$

$$\text{where: } g_{iT}(\theta) = \frac{1}{T} \sum_{t=1}^{T} h_i(x_{t+1}, \theta) \otimes z_t$$

A simple monte carlo experiment illustrates the sensitivity of the parameter estimates. The data generation process is simple. Each period's disturbance term, $h(x_t, \theta)$, and return, R_{t+1} , are generated independently using lognormal distributions. Together with specific values for α and β, the disturbances and returns determine consumption. Consumption is constructed as if the first formulation were true.[6] Three instruments are included: a constant and single lags of the return and of the ratio of consumption across periods. That is:

$$z_t = \{1, R_{t-1}, \frac{C_t}{C_{t-1}}\}.$$

So, there are three moment conditions for each formulation of the disturbance term. For each formulation, the three moment conditions first are weighted equally to give initial parameter estimates. The initial estimates then are used to calculate new weights, W_{1T} and W_{2T}, for constructing the objective function. Finally, the objective function is minimized to give the final Generalized method of moments estimators.[7]

Estimators are constructed for sample sizes ranging from 30 to 5000, using a risk aversion parameter of -0.80 and a discount rate of 0.95.[8] Table 14 summarizes the results of 1000 repetitions of this exercise. The first two columns of the table give the mean values of the Generalized method of moments estimators using the two formulations of the moment conditions. As the columns

Table 14

GMM Estimates

$$h_1(x_t,\theta) = \beta(\frac{C_{t+1}}{C_t})^{\alpha}R_{t+1} - 1 \qquad and \quad h_2(x_t,\theta) = (\frac{C_{t+1}}{C_t})^{\alpha}R_{t+1} - \frac{1}{\beta}$$

$\alpha = -0.80 \quad \beta = 0.95$

	Mean Estimates		Difference	Tests of Equality
	$\bar{\theta}_1$	$\bar{\theta}_2$	$\bar{\theta}_1 - \bar{\theta}_2$	H_o: $\bar{\theta}_{1i} - \bar{\theta}_{2i} = 0$
Sample Size = 30				
$\bar{\alpha}$	-0.398	-0.494	0.096	7.500
	(0.013)	(0.006)	(0.013)	
$\bar{\beta}$	0.843	1.437	-0.594	-13.560
	(0.009)	(0.042)	(0.044)	
Sample Size = 100				
$\bar{\alpha}$	-0.532	-0.479	-0.053	-3.410
	(0.017)	(0.004)	(0.015)	
$\bar{\beta}$	0.886	1.227	-0.341	-23.020
	(0.007)	(0.014)	(0.015)	
Sample Size = 500				
$\bar{\alpha}$	-0.627	-0.489	-0.138	-13.940
	(0.012)	(0.004)	(0.010)	
$\bar{\beta}$	0.885	1.095	-0.209	-32.800
	(0.006)	(0.002)	(0.006)	

(continues)

Table 14--continued
GMM Estimates

$$h_1(x_t,\theta) = \beta(\frac{C_{t+1}}{C_t})^{\alpha}R_{t+1} - 1 \quad and \quad h_2(x_t,\theta) = (\frac{C_{t+1}}{C_t})^{\alpha}R_{t+1} - \frac{1}{\beta}$$

$\alpha = -0.80 \quad \beta = 0.95$

	Mean Estimates $\bar{\theta}_1$	$\bar{\theta}_2$	Difference $\bar{\theta}_1 - \bar{\theta}_2$	Tests of Equality H_o: $\bar{\theta}_{1i} - \bar{\theta}_{2i} = 0$
Sample Size = 1000				
$\bar{\alpha}$	-0.657	-0.498	-0.159	-18.320
	(0.010)	(0.004)	(0.009)	
$\bar{\beta}$	0.888	1.068	-0.180	-30.220
	(0.006)	(0.002)	(0.006)	
Sample Size = 5000				
$\bar{\alpha}$	-0.625	-0.471	-0.154	-31.520
	(0.007)	(0.003)	(0.005)	
$\bar{\beta}$	0.968	1.048	-0.080	-23.440
	(0.003)	(0.001)	(0.003)	

Notes:
1. The number of iterations equals 1000.
2. Standard deviations are in parentheses.
3. The final column gives t-statistics. The hypotheses that the parameter estimates are equal are rejected at any conventional significance level.

show, the parameter estimates only slowly approach their underlying values. The estimate of the risk aversion parameter is particularly bad when the"wrong" formulation is used, even when the sample size equals 5000.

Differences between the mean parameter estimates using the two formulations, along with the sample standard deviations of those differences, are given in the next column. For the risk aversion parameter, the differences actually increase as the sample size increases. The increase reflects the improvement of the estimates constructed using the "correct" formulation relative to the performance under the alternative formulation. For the discount rate, the difference between the estimates declines with sample size; but even with a sample size of 5000, a difference persists. The last column gives the statistics testing the hypotheses that the estimates are the same under the two formulations.[9] For each parameter, and in every sample size, the hypothesis that the estimates are the same is rejected at any conventional significance level.

CONCLUSIONS

That these estimates differ significantly illustrates that the apparently arbitrary formulation choice is a consequential one: to adopt a formulation is to adopt an estimator. In this example, the two formulations are theoretically indistinct. In practice, one formulation may be superior to the other; however, knowledge of that superiority requires additional distributional or structural information that is not given here.[10] Without such information, other dramatically different specifications and correspondingly dramatic estimates cannot be excluded either. For example, while this section has examined $R(\theta) = \beta^{-1}$, it instead might have examined $R(\theta) = \beta^{m}$, where *m* is very large or very small![11] Without additional restrictions, the generalized method of moments procedure gives rise to many such formulations and estimators.

The sensitivity of generalized method of moments estimates reflects the familiar difficulty, arising in many estimation problems, of choosing a specific functional form. Since a unique generalized method of moments estimator requires choosing a specific functional form of the moment conditions, it imposes, explicitly or implicitly, specific distributional and structural assumptions. These assumptions are problematic in precisely those applications where the use of generalized method of moments has been most notable: where structural and distributional knowledge has been viewed as unsatisfactory.

NOTES

1. The moment conditions may appear more familiar when written as $E_t[f(x_t, z_t, \theta)] = 0$, where z_t is a vector of instruments. However, that extra notation is not needed in this section of the paper.

2. For example, let $R(\theta) = \theta_i^m$. Then,

$$f_a(x_t, \theta) \quad = \quad \theta_i^m \bullet f(x_t, \theta).$$

3. Hansen shows that the weighting matrix minimizing the asymptotic covariance of the estimator is the inverse of the asymptotic covariance of the sample moments. It is estimated initially using a preliminary, consistent estimate of the parameters (θ_o) to construct a sample covariance matrix. In the simplest case, without serial correlation, and using the same preliminary parameter estimate, θ_o:

$$W_{ga} \quad = \quad [\frac{1}{T}\sum_{t=1}^{T} f_a(x_t, \theta_o)f_a(x_t, \theta_o)'\,]^{-1} \quad =$$

$$R(\theta_o)^{-2}\,[\frac{1}{T}\sum_{t=1}^{T} f(x_t, \theta_o)f(x_t, \theta_o)'\,]^{-1} \quad = \quad R(\theta_o)^{-2}\;W_g.$$

4. The first term of FOC 2, $\left(\frac{\partial g_{aT}}{\partial \theta}\right)'$, may be expanded by recalling that $g_{aT} = R(\theta) \bullet g_T$; so, it becomes:

$$\left(\frac{\partial g_{aT}}{\partial \theta}\right)' = \left|\frac{\partial R(\theta)}{\partial \theta}\cdot g_T + R(\theta)\cdot\frac{\partial g_T}{\partial \theta}\right|' .$$

The second term of FOC 2, W_{ga}, is the Generalized method of moments weighting matrix:

$$W_{ga} = R(\theta_o)^{-2}\ W_g.$$

The third term of FOC 2 ($g_{a,T}$) equals $R(\theta)\bullet g_T$. Rearranged, these give FOC 2'.

5. Using the previous notation, $R(\theta) = \beta^{-1}$.

6. For each period, two pseudo random variables, v_{1t} and v_{2t}, are generated independently as standard normal variables using the GAUSS "RNDN" routine. The hypothesized disturbance term, $h(x_t,\theta)$, and the return, R, are simple transformations of those variables:

$$h(x_t, \theta) = \exp(v_{1t} - \frac{1}{2}) - 1,$$
$$\text{and } R_{t+1} = \exp(v_{2t}).$$

Together with values for α and β, these variables determine the ratio of consumption across periods. When $h_1(x_t,\theta)$ is the underlying disturbance term (as it is in Hansen and Singleton):

$$\frac{C_{t+1}}{C_t} = \left[\frac{h(x_t,\theta)+1}{\beta R_{t+1}}\right]^{\frac{1}{\alpha}}.$$

7. The function is minimized using the GAUSS module "OPTMUM" and the Newton-Raphson algorithm. Analytical derivatives and hessians are constructed for each formulation. The "true" parameter values are given as starting values for the minimization.

8. Hansen and Singleton report estimates of the risk aversion parameter of about -0.90 to about -0.50 and of the discount rate of about 0.99 to 1.00.

9. Each test statistic is simply the difference divided by its sample standard deviation.

10. Knowledge of the correct formulation is equivalent to knowledge of the distribution. In such cases maximum likelihood estimation sometimes can be used.

11. In the context of the Wald statistic, LaFontaine and White (1986) note that making such a non-linear transformation of a hypothesis is a way of "Obtaining Any Wald Statistic You Want." Here, the parameter estimate is of interest: simulations with m=100 yielded estimates of β of as large as 45.0.

References

Adler, M. and B. Dumas. International Portfolio Choices and Corporate Finace: A Synthesis, *Journal Of Finance*. 38:925-84. 1983.

Aliber, R. The Interest Parity Theorem: A Reinterpretation, *Journal of Political Economy*,81:6, 1451-9. 1987.

Bank for International Settlements. *60th Annual Report,* Basle, 149-154. June 11, 1990.

Bicksler, A. and A. Chen. An Economic Analysis of Interest Rate Swaps, *Journal of Finance*,41:3, 645-655. 1986.

Bonser-Neal, C., G. Brauer, R. Neal and S. Wheatley. International Investment Restrictions and Closed-End Country Fund Prices. *Journal of Finance.* 45:523-48. 1990.

Branson, W. The Minimum Covered Interest Differential Needed for International Arbitrage Activity, *Journal of Political Economy*, 1028-1037. 1969.

Campbell, J. Stock Returns and the Term Structure, *Journal of Financial Economics* 18, 373-399. 1987.

Campbell, J. and R. Clarida. The Term Structure of Euromarket Interest Rates, an Empirical Investigation, *Journal of Monetary Economics* 19, 25-44. 1987.

Campbell, J. and Y. Hamao. Predictable Stock Returns in the United States and Japan: A Study of Long-Term Capital Market Integration. National Bureau of Economic Research Working Paper No. 3191. 1989.

Clinton, K. Transactions Costs and Covered Interest Arbitrage: Theory and Evidence, *Journal of Political Economy*, 96:2, 358-70. 1988.

Cox, J., J. Ingersoll and S. Ross. A Theory of the Term Structure of Interest Rates, *Econometrica* 53, 385-408. 1985.

Cumby, R.E. Is It Risk? Explaining Deviations from Uncovered Interest Parity, *Journal of Monetary Economics.* 22:279-300. 1988.

Cumby, R.E. Consumption Risk and International Equity Returns: Some Empirical Evidence, *Journal of International Money and Finance.* 9:181-92. 1990.

Cumby, R. E., and M. Obstfeld. A Note on Exchange Rate Expectations and Nominal Interest Differentials: A Test of the Fisher Hypothesis, *Journal of Finance.* 36:697-703. 1981.

Cumby, R. E. and M. Obstfeld. International Interest Rate and Price-Level Linkages: A Review of Recent Evidence, in J. F. Bilson and R. C.Marston, eds., *Exchange Rate Theory and Practice.* Chicago, Ill.: University of Chicago Press. 1984.

Dooley, M., and P. Isard. Capital Controls, Political Risk, and Deviations from Interest Rate Parity, *Journal of Political Economy*, 88:2, 70-84. 1980.

Estrella, A., and G. Hardouvelis. The Term Structure as a Predictor of Real Economic Activity, Federal Reserve Bank of New York Working Paper No. 89-07. 1989.

Feldstein, M. and C. Horioka. Domestic Savings and International CapitalFlows, *Economic Lournal* 90(June): 314-29.1980.

Frankel, J. Quantifying International Capital Mobility. in D. Bernheim and J. Shoven, eds. *National Saving and Economic Performance*. University of Chicago Press, Chicago, 227-260. 1991.

Frankel, J. Liberalization of Korea's Foreign Exchange Markets, Pacific Basin Working Paper No. PB92-08, Center for Pacific Basin Monetary and Economic Studies, Economic Research Department, Federal Reserve Bank of San Francisco. March 1992.

Frankel, J. and A. MacArthur. Political vs. Currency Premia in International Real Interest Differentials: A Study of Forward Rates for 24 Countries, *European Economic Review*, 32, 1083-1121. 1988.

Frankel, J. and C. Okongwu. Liberalized Portfolio Capital Inflows in Emerging Markets: Sterilization, Expectations, and the Incompleteness of Interest Rate Convergence, NBER Working Paper No. 5156, June 1995.

Frankel, J., S. Phillips, and M. Chinn. Financial and Currency Integration in the European Monetary System: The Statistical Record, in F. Torres and F. Giavazzi, eds, *The Transition to Economic and Monetary Union in Europe*. Banco do Portugal, Lisbon, and Centre for Economic Policy Research, London. 1990.

Giavazzi, F. and M. Pagano. Capital Controls and the European Monetary System, Euromobilaiare, Occasional Paper, 1985.

Giovannini A. and P. Jorion. Interest Rates and Risk Premia in the Stock Market and the Foreign Exchange Market, *Journal of International Money and Finance* 6, 107-123. 1987.

Golub, S. S. International Capital Mobility: Net versus Gross Stocks and Flows, *Journal of International Money and Finance* 9 (December): 424-39. 1990.

Gregory, A. and M. Veall. Formulating Wald Tests of Nonlinear Restrictions, *Econometrica* 53, p.1465. 1985.

Hansen, L. P., Large Sample Properties of Generalized Method of Moments Estimators, *Econometrica*, Vol. 50, No. 4, P. 1029. 1982.

Hansen, L. and R. Hodrick. Forward Exchange Rates as Optimal Predictors of the Future Spot Rate: an Econometric Analysis, *Journal of Political Economy* 88, 829-853. 1980.

Hansen, L. and R. Hodrick. Risk Averse Speculation in the Forward Foreign Exchange Market: an Econometric Analysis of Linear Models, in J. Frenkel, ed., *Exchange Rates and International Macroeconomics*, University of Chicago Press, Chicago, 115-152. 1983.

Hansen, L.P. and K.J. Singleton. Generalized Instrumental Variables of Nonlinear Rational Expectations Models, *Econometrica*, Vol. 50, No 5, p. 1269. 1982.

Hansen, L. and K. Singleton. Stochastic Consumption, Risk Aversion the Temporal Behavior of Asset Returns, *Journal of Political Economy* 91, 249-65. 1983.

Harvey, C. The World Price of Covariance Risk, *The Journal of Finance* 46, 111-157. 1991.

Hodrick, R. *The Empirical Evidence on the Efficiency of Forward and Futures Foreign Exchange Markets*, Harwood Academic Publishers, London. 1987.

Hodrick, R. and S. Srivastava. An Investigation of Risk and Return in Forward Foreign Exchange, *Journal of International Money and Finance* 3, 5-29. 1984.

Kasman, B., and C. Pigott. Interest Rate Divergences among the Major Industrial Nations, Federal Reserve Bank of New York *Quarterly Review*, 16, 28-46. 1988.

Lafontaine, F. and K. White. Obtaining Any Wald Statistic You Want, *Economics Letters* 21, p.35-40. 1986.

Lewis, K. The Behavior of Eurocurrency Returns Across Different Holding Periods and Monetary Regimes, *Journal of Finance* 45, 1211-1236. 1990.

Lewis, K. Puzzles in International Financial Markets, National Bureau of Economic Research, Working Paper No. 4951. 1994.

Lucas, R. Econometric Policy Evaluation: A Critique, in *The Phillips Curve and Labor Markets*, K. Brunner and A.H. Meltzer, eds., Carnegie-Rochester Conference Series on Public Policy 1. Amsterdam, North-Holland. 1976.

Lucas, R. Asset Prices in an Exchange Economy, *Econometrica* 46, 1429-45. 1978.

McCormick, F, Covered Interest Arbitrage: Unexploited Profits? Comment, *Journal of Political Economy*, 87:2, 411-417. 1979.

Newey, W. and K. West. A Simple, Positive Semi-definite, Heteroskedasticity and Autocorrelation Consistent Covariance Matrix, *Econometrica* 55, 703-708. 1987.

Obstfeld, M. How Integrated are World Capital Markets? Some New Tests. National Bureau of Economic Research Working Paper No. 2075. 1986.

Obstfeld, M. International Capital Market Mobility in the 1990s, in P.B. Kenen, ed., *Understanding Interdependence: The Macroeconomics of the Open Economy*, Princeton University Press, Princeton, NJ. 1994.

Paredes, C. E. Epilogue: In the Aftermath of Hyperinflation, in *Peru's Path to Recovery*, Carlos E. Predes and Jeffrey D. Sachs, eds. The Brookings Institution, Washington D.C. 1991.

Phillips, P.C.B. and J. Park, On the Formulation of Wald Tests of Nonlinear Restrictions, *Econometrica* 56, 1065-1083. 1988.

Popper, H. Formulating Non-linear Moment Conditions of Generalized Method of Moments Estimators, Working Paper, Santa Clara University. 1994.

Popper, H. Term Premia Comovement in German, Japanese, and U.S. Domestic Markets, *Open Economies Review*, 6. 1995

Popper, H.Long-Term Covered Interest Parity: Evidence from Currency Swaps, *Journal of International Money and Finance* 12, 439-448. 1993.

Salomon Brothers, *International Bond Market Roundup,* New York, weekly, 1985-1988.

Shigehara, Kumiharu. Japan's Experience with the Use of Monetary Policy and the Process of Liberalization, Working Paper, Bank of Japan. 1990.

Shiller, F., J. Campbell and K. Shoenholtz. Forward Rates and Future Policy: Interpreting the Term Structure of Interest Rates, *Brookings Papers on Economic Activity* 1, 173-217. 1983.

Shiller, R. and J. McCulloch. The Term Structure of Interest Rates, National Bureau of Economic Research Working Paper No. 2341. 1987

Stock, J., and M. Watson. Business Cycle Properties of Selected U.S. Economic Time Series, 1959-1988. National Bureau of Economic Research Working Paper No. 3376. 1990.

Summers, L. Tax Policy and International Competitiveness, in *International Aspects of Financial Policies*, J. Frenkel ed., University of Chicago Press, Chicago. 1988.

Takezawa, Nobuya. Currency Swaps and Long-Term Covered Interest Parity, *Economics Letters*, 49, 181-185. 1995.

Taylor, A.M. International Capital Mobility in History: The Saving Investment Relationship, National Bureau of Economic Research Working Paper No. 5743. 1996.

Taylor, M., Covered Interest Parity: A High-Frequency, High-Quality Data Study, *Econometrica,*54, 429-38. 1987.

Tesar, L. Savings, Investment and International Capital Flows, *Journal of International Economics* 31:55-78. 1991.

Thorbecke, Erik. *Adjustment and Equity in Indonesia*, OECD Development Center Studies, Paris, 1992.

Turnovsky, S.J. The Term Structure of Interest Rates and the Effects of Macroeconomics Policy, *Journal of Money, Credit, and Banking* 21, 321-347. 1989.

White, H. A Heteroskedasticity-Consistent Covariance Matrix Estimator and a Direct Test for Heteroskedasticity, *Econometrica* 48. 1980.

Index

Aliber, Robert, 29
Arbitrage, 8, 9, 15, 16, 20, 29
Asia, 5

Bahrain, 30
Bank for International Settlements, 30

Canada, x, 15, 16, 21, 32
Capital Asset Pricing, 7, 38
  model, 38, 39, 42, 49
Capital Controls, 9, 26
Constant Risk Premium, 46
Covered Interest Parity, vii-11, 16-21, 26, 28, 31
Cross-Currency Interest Rate Swap, see Currency Swap
Currency Swap, vii, x, 11, 16, 18, 19, 30, 46

Default Risk, 20
Deregulation, see Financial Deregulation

Euromarket, ix, 15
Europe, 5
European Monetary System, 30
Exchange Rate
  Forward, 17
  Spot, 9
  Risk, 28
Expectation,
  Errors, 40
  Hypothesis, 46

Feldstein, Martin, 6, 7, 29
Financial Deregulation, 4, 37
Foreign Exchange Swap, 16, 18
Forward Contract, 9, 10, 18
Forward Exchange Contract, see forward contract
France, 4, 5 , 30
Frankel, Jeffrey A., 8, 10, 17, 26, 32

Generalized Method of Moments, vii, 64
Germany, 5, 16
Giavazzi, Francesco, 26
Greece, 30
Gregory, Allan, 61, 65

Hansen, Lars P., 38
Hedging, 16
Hodrick, Robert, 38
Horioka, Charles, 6, 7, 29

India, 5
Inflation, 8, 9
Information Variables, 41, 42
Interest Parity, 37
  Covered, 8
  Nominal, 8
  Real, 8
  Swap-Covered, 19, 20
  Uncovered, 8
Interest Rate Swap, 19
Investment, 6
  and Saving, see Feldstein, Martin and Horioka, Charles

Japan. , xi

Korea, 5

Latent variable, xi, 38-43, 49, 50, 57, 58
Latin America, 5
Less Developed Countries, 17
Lewis, Karen 38, 42

McCormick, Frank, 5, 33
Mean Absolute Deviations, 24
Method of Moments, vii, 63, 64, 67-74, 77, 78
Mexico, 30
Moment Conditions, 63, 67-74
Monte Carlo, xiii, 8, 57
Moving Average Error, 42

Netherlands, 30
Non-Linear Transformation, xi

OECD countries, 6
Offshore Markets, 5, 17
Omitted Variables, 6
Onshore Markets, 15, 17, 20, 21, 23, 24, 49, 50
Orthogonality Conditions, xi, 63, 67-74
Overlapping Observations, 42
Pagano, Marco 26, 37
Parity Conditions, see Interest Parity
Political Jurisdiction, 16, 50
Political Risk, 8, 20
Power, 42
Proportionality Restrictions, 40, 42

Purchasing Power Parity, 9

Real Interest Parity, 8, 9
Realignments, 30
Reduced Form Coefficients, 40
Representative Consumer, 72
Risk, 17, 18, 37
  Aversion, 77
  Currency, 18
  Default, 20
Root Mean Square Error, 23

Sample Standard Deviations, 26
Saving and Investment Correlations, 6
Serial Correlation, 33
Simulteneity, 7
Singleton, Kenneth, 65
South Africa, 30
Stabilization Packages, 5
Swap-Covered Interest Parity, 19, 20
Switzerland, x, 16

Term Premium, 41-43
Term Spread, 42
Term Structure, 46

Uncovered interest parity, see Interest Parity
United Kingdom, 5, 16
United States, 4

Variance, 28
Veall, Michael, 61, 65

Wald Statistic, 46, 49, 50
Withholding Taxes, 4

9781138566811